LOOM
KNITTING
SCARVES, HATS, BAGS & MORE

LOOM
KNITTING
SCARVES, HATS, BAGS & MORE

41 SIMPLE AND SNUGGLY NO-NEEDLE DESIGNS FOR ALL LOOM KNITTERS

ISELA PHELPS

St. Martin's Griffin
New York

LOOM KNITTING SCARVES, HATS,
BAGS & MORE. Copyright © 2011
by Quintet Publishing Limited. All
rights reserved. Printed in China. For
information, address St. Martin's Press,
175 Fifth Avenue, New York,
N.Y. 10010.

www.stmartins.com

This book was designed and
produced by
Quintet Publishing Limited,
6 Blundell Street
London N7 9BH, UK

Art Director: Michael Charles
Designer: Bonnie Bryan
Photography: David Murphy
Illustrator: Bernard Chau
Project Editor: Anya Hayes
Managing Editor: Donna Gregory
Publisher: Mark Searle

Printed in China by 1010 Printing
International Limited

Library of Congress Cataloging-in-
Publication Data Available Upon Request

ISBN 978-0-312-59140-3

First U.S. Edition: January 2012

10 9 8 7 6 5 4 3 2 1

Contents

Introduction

Hello again my dear loom knitters, it is a pleasure to share with you this latest endeavor, *Loom Knitting Scarves, Hats, Bags & More.* It makes a great addition to the Loom Knitting Primer series. In this book, we have included a collection of designs ranging from simple hats to amazing lacy shawls. The collection of designs ranges in levels of expertise from beginner to advanced, keeping in mind our diverse readership. As always, we encourage you to use our ideas in this book as inspiration to launch you into a creative realm.

We have listened to your requests and in this edition we have included the most popularly available knitting looms, the Knifty Knitter® Looms by Provo Craft. You will find that over 90 percent of the projects were completed using these widely available knitting looms, visit your local craft store and chances are that you will find the knitting looms we used in this project.

Inside the first few chapters, new loom knitters will be guided through the basics of Loom Knitting with step-by-step illustrations and instructions. Seasoned loom knitters can dive right in at Chapter 4, where they will be met with fresh and challenging designs. We hope the collection within these pages inspires you to pick up your knitting looms again and create something wonderful for yourself and your loved ones.

Keep those looms turning, and until next time!

Isela Phelps

Reading the Patterns

Find all the materials and pattern information on a handy side bar. On the side bar, you will find the knitting loom needed, yarn, notions, and even information on gauge.

Loom

Materials

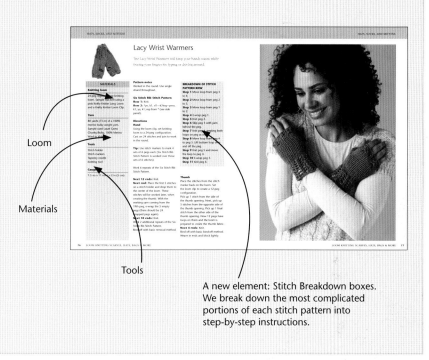

Tools

A new element: Stitch Breakdown boxes. We break down the most complicated portions of each stitch pattern into step-by-step instructions.

Pattern style in this book

The patterns in the book are written in a short format to save on space and may look unfamiliar. Here is an example:

You will see:
CO 24sts, join to work in the round.
Work in 2x2 Rib stitch for 1 in. (2.5 cm).
Work in St st. until leg measures 6 in. (15 cm) from CO edge.

It means:
Cast on 24 stitches/pegs. Connect the last stitch to the first stitch to prepare to knit in rounds.
Knit 2 stitches/pegs, purl 2 stitches/pegs, repeat the sequence around the loom until you reach the end of the round. Repeat the entire sequence until you have 1 inch (2.5 cm) of work.
Switch to stockinette stitch (knit all rounds) and knit until you reach 6 inches (15 cm) from the cast-on edge.

You will find a list of symbols and abbreviations on page 140.

Pattern presentation

*: used to mark the beginning of a repeated section.
You will see:
*k1, p1; rep from * to the end of round.

It means:
k1, p1, k1, p1, k1, p1.....

( ): used to include different sizes that can be knitted from the pattern, for example S (M, L, XL). Before beginning your pattern, highlight all the instructions for the size you are following.

Projects for You to Try

52 Flat Panel Scarf

52 Green Scarf

52 & 74 Pom-pom Scarf & Mittens

54 Adamaris Shawl

56 Symphony Lace Cowl

58 Firefly Scarf

60 Carys Shrug

62 CrossOver Wrap

66 Bluebells Hat

76
Lacy Wrist
warmers

67 Ribbed Beanie

68 Iris Beanie

70 Cloverleaf Slipper Socks

72 Twilled Slipper Socks

74 Family of Mittens

80 Bunny Hat

82 Little Duckling Hat

84 Little Lamb Hat

86 Baby's First Mitts and Socks

88 Braid Circular Blanket

90 Stroller Baby Blanket

98 Flowers Felted Bag

100 Starry Night Bag

102 Lexi Bag

104 Knick-knack Boxes

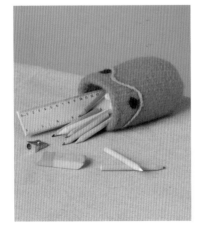

106 Pencil Holder

108 Cell Phone Cozy

112 Aran Lapghan

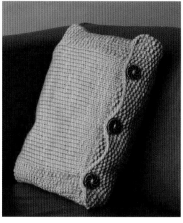

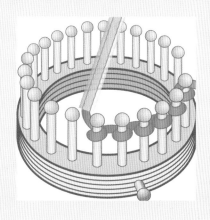

CHAPTER 1
Materials
and Tools

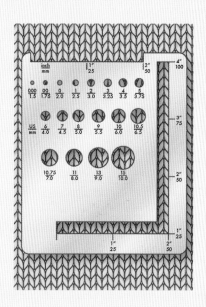

In this chapter we look at looms and other essentials
for your knitting bag, plus yarn weights.

Knitting Looms

Knitting looms are available in all sorts of shapes and sizes, and with different gauges/sets. This book uses a variety of knitting looms, all of which are available at your local craft store and/or through online stores.

Collecting knitting looms, like needles, can become expensive, especially if you want to have each size available at your disposal. Before purchasing one, make a list of the qualities that you are looking for—assess your needs and see which loom can best fulfil them.

- Overall durability: Will it break on the first or second use? If your dog happens to use it as a chew toy will it survive the game?
- Wood or plastic base: Does the base need any upkeep?
- Gauge of the loom: Will it allow you to knit with the yarns you use the most?

- Type of peg: Is a smooth peg what you are looking for? Or do you want a bit of resistance? If you happen to step on it, can the peg be replaced?
- Do the pegs have grooves to facilitate picking up the loops?
- Do the pegs have a knob at the top to prevent the yarn from accidentally popping off?

Your knitting looms are your main tools to create your knits; finding the right one will take a little time and research.

Loom gauge table

Yarn recommended	1 SUPER FINE	2 FINE	3 LIGHT	4 MEDIUM	5 BULKY	6 SUPER BULKY
Distance from center of pin to center of pin in inches	3/16	1/4	3/8–3/7	1/2	5/8–3/4	4/5
Loom gauge	Extra Fine Gauge	Fine Gauge	Small Gauge	Regular Gauge	Large Gauge	ExtraLarge Gauge
Manufacturers	EFG	FG	SG	RG	LG	ELG
• CindiWood Looms			•	•	•	•
• Décor Accents, Inc.	•	•	•	•	•	•
• In the Attic				•		
• Knifty Knitter Long Loom Series			•			
• Knifty Knitter Round Loom Series					•	•
• Kiss Looms			•	•	•	•
• Knitting Board Company		•	•	•		

Quick reference

Large gauge knitting looms

- Distance from center of peg to center of peg: ⅝ inch +
- **Available in:** Wood and plastic, with nylon pegs, plastic, wood, and metal
- **Yarn:** Bulky weight yarns or two strands of medium weight yarns
- **Knits:** Bulky weight knits and knits that will be felted
- **Gauge:** Approximately 1½–2 stitches per inch
- Compared to needle knitting stitch gauge: size 13 (9 mm)

Regular gauge knitting looms

- Distance from center of peg to center of peg: ½ inch
- **Available in:** Wood and plastic, with nylon pegs, plastic, wood, and metal
- **Yarn:** Chunky weight yarns or two strands of sport weight yarn
- **Knits:** Medium weight knits
- **Gauge:** Approximately 3–3½ stitches per inch
  Compared to needle knitting stitch gauge: size 10 (6 mm)

Small gauge knitting looms

- Distance from center of peg to center of peg: ⅜–³/₇ inch
- **Available in:** Wood and plastic, with nylon pegs, plastic, wood, and metal
- **Yarn:** Worsted weight/medium weight yarn
- **Knits:** Medium and lightweight knits
- **Gauge:** Approximately 3½–4 stitches per inch
- Compared to needle knitting stitch gauge: size 7–8 (4.5–5 mm)

Fine gauge knitting looms

- Distance from center of peg to center of peg: ¼ inch
- **Available in:** Wood base and metal pins/pegs
- **Yarn:** Sport weight/DK weight
- **Knits:** Lightweight knits
- **Gauge:** Approximately 4–5 stitches per inch
  Compared to needle knitting stitch gauge: size 5–6 (3.75–4 mm)

Extra fine gauge knitting looms

- Distance from center of peg to center of peg: ³/₁₆ inch
- **Available in:** Wood base and metal pins/pegs
- **Yarn:** Fingering weight/sock weight
- **Knits:** Lightweight knits
- **Gauge:** Approximately 7–8 stitches per inch
- Compared to needle knitting stitch gauge: size 1–2 (2.25–2.75 mm)

The knitting hook or knitting tool is available in two different tips: one with a blunt tip and one with a sharper tip. The blunt-tip knitting tool is recommended when working with worsted weight to chunky weight yarn. The sharper-tip knitting tool works best when using a finer yarn such as fingering weight or sock weight yarn.

**Provo Craft®
Knifty Knitters
Long Loom Series**

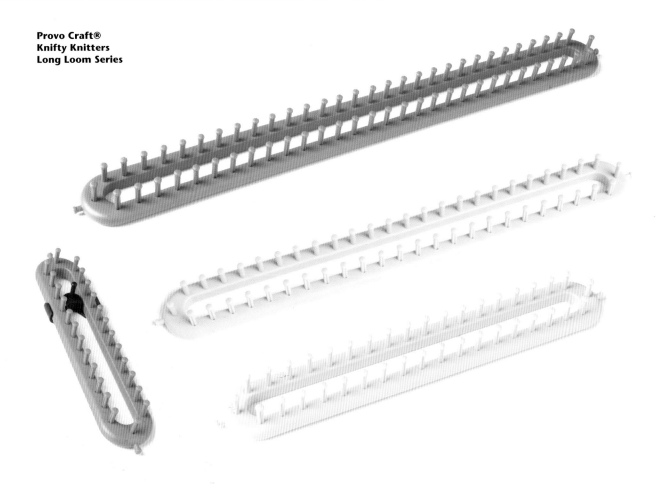

A variety of knitting looms were used to complete the projects in this book. Let's take a look at some of them and list their characteristics.

Provo Craft® Knifty Knitters Long Loom Series:
a set of four knitting looms, 22 inch (blue), 18 inch (green), 14 inch (yellow) and the 10 inch (pink).

22" Long Loom (Blue) 30 sets plus 2 end pegs/ 62 pegs total
18" Long Loom (Green) 24 set plus 2 end pegs/ 50 pegs total
14" Long Loom (Yellow) 18 sets plus 2 end pegs/ 38 pegs total
10" Long Loom (Pink) 12 sets plus 2 end pegs/ 26 pegs total

Loom Clip—used in conjunction with the Long Loom Series knitting looms to create smaller tubes.

Provo Craft® Round Loom Series,
a set of 4 knitting looms (pictured at right).

Extra Large Round Loom (Yellow) 41 pegs
Large Round Loom (Green) 36 pegs
Medium Round Loom (Red) 31 pegs
Small Round Loom (Blue) 24 pegs

Provo Craft® Adult Hat Loom, sold as single loom
Adult Hat Loom (Purple) 48 pegs (pictured right)

**Provo Craft®
Hat Loom**

**Provo Craft®
Round Loom Series**

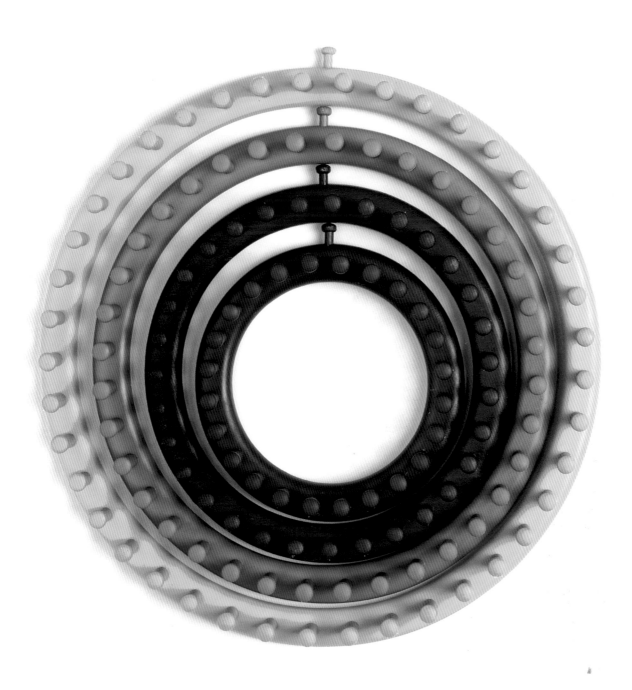

Let's Talk Gauge

Let's take a small break and look at some numbers. Don't be scared and run away, but do feel free to reach for a little chocolate to calm your nerves. It's not algebra, honest.

When following a pattern, matching the gauge is imperative, unless fit is not a factor. For this reason alone, it is recommended to always knit a swatch before embarking on any project—especially if the project needs to fit a certain someone.

Let's make a swatch

To loom knit a swatch, cast on the number of stitches as called for in the gauge section of the pattern plus 10 more. If the gauge for the pattern states 4 stitches over 2 inches (5 cm), then cast on 14 stitches. Loom knit the swatch on the stitch pattern called for in the pattern. When the swatch reaches about 6 inches (15 cm) in length bind off.

To measure for gauge, count all stitches—¼ stitches and ½ stitches count! Measure in a few different places to make sure that the gauge is consistent.

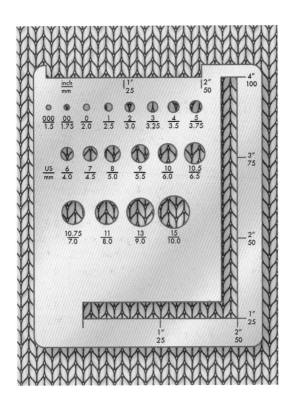

Got gauge—you can go forth and start loom knitting! Count yourself lucky!

More stitches per inch than called for in the pattern.
What does this mean? It means that if you knit with this yarn and knitting loom the item may be too small.
Fixer-uppers:
• Try with a thicker yarn.
• Try with a larger gauge knitting loom.

Fewer stitches per inch than called for in the pattern. What does this mean? It means that if you are stoic enough to continue, you will end up with an item that may be big enough to fit Goliath!
Fixer-uppers:
• Try with a thinner yarn.
• Try a smaller gauge knitting loom.

Look at the stitch gauge guide (left). If you don't have one, you can also use a measuring tape. Knit a small swatch to try out the stitches. Set it on a flat surface. Set your stitch guide in the center of your swatch. Align your stitch guide so there is a row aligned to the horizontal part of the L-shaped window.

Count the number of stitches along the horizontal side of the L-shaped window. Write the number down. Count the rows along the vertical side of the L-shaped window. Write down the number. The numbers that you come up with are your gauge for that loom, using the type of yarn in the project, and the stitch used in the project. In this diagram, for example, there are 10 stitches across and 19 rows.

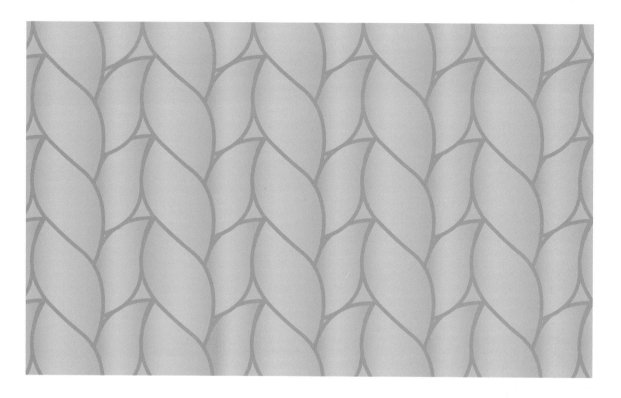

Gauge is dependent upon four factors:
- Yarn
- Gauge of the knitting loom
- Type of stitch
- Your personal wrapping tension

The three first elements will have the most impact upon gauge. If any of these three elements change, the gauge will change.

Playing with numbers

If your heart is set on a specific yarn but you still don't get gauge, don't despair. Bring out the calculator and do some math to calculate the number of stitches and rows you will need to create the same item.

Let's assume you want to knit a square that is 20 x 20 in (51 x 51 cm). The gauge given in the pattern is 6 stitches and 8 rows in 2 inches (5 cm).

To create the square with the gauge above you will need to cast on 60 stitches and knit for 80 rows. But, your swatch tells you that you've got a gauge of 4 stitches and 6 rows in 2 inches.

To create the square of 20 x 20 in (51 x 51 cm) you will need to make the following changes: Cast on 40 pegs and knit 60 rows.

Essential Tools for Your Loomy Bag

The journey is about to begin and, like any journey, you need to gather your tools and gear up to make the journey easier and more enjoyable.

A Knitting Tool, Hook or Pick is the most essential gadget for the loom knitter—you can never have enough of them. Have a few of them on hand. If you are a worrywart like me, you will have a drawer full, as they are sneaky and tend to hide when you need them the most.

 The purpose of the knitting tool is to facilitate knitting on the knitting looms. The tool allows you to lift the yarn up and over the peg, creating a stitch. A knitting tool is similar to a dental pick or nut pick, and is generally made out of metal, with a wood or plastic handle. The end is bent at an angle to allow the lifting of the stitches. Knitting tools come with different ends: some sharp for use when knitting on very small pegs and fingering weight yarns and some more blunt for use with bigger pegs and thicker yarns.

 If you happen to lose all your knitting tools, you can also use a small crochet hook, nut pick, or even an orange peeler.

The yarn guide/aid is a thin plastic tube. It facilitates wrapping the yarn around the pegs and helps maintain an even tension in your wrapping. Some knitting loom vendors carry them as part of their line; if you are unable to find one, you can easily make one (see box below).

A stitch gauge guide allows you to determine exactly the number of stitches and rows per inch in your work. It is a flat metal or plastic piece with ruler markings on the sides. In the center there is a small L-shaped window that allows you to check the rows and stitches per inch of the knitted piece. If you don't have one, you could make one out of stiff card.

 To check the gauge, block the knitted piece lightly and place it on a flat surface. Now place the stitch gauge guide on top of it. Line the bottom window opening with one row of the knitted piece. Line one of the columns of stitches to the side as shown. To determine the gauge, count the stitches per inch in the window opening. Count also the rows per inch. Make sure to count ¼ stitches and ½ stitches.

Scissors/Yarn Cutters are invaluable. Some yarns are easy to break with your hands, but you will find that many synthetic yarns and cottons are almost impossible to break. Carrying small scissors in your knitting bag is always advisable. If traveling by airplane, I recommend obtaining a yarn/thread cutter that you can take along with you.

A Row Counter is a nifty item to have in your knitter's bag. It comes in handy… as long as you don't

How to make a yarn guide

1 Find a ballpoint pen with a hollow center.
2 Take out the inside ink cartridge.
3 Cut the tip off the barrel.
4 Sand any rough spots with an emery board.
5 Pass the starting tail of the yarn through and wrap it around the pegs with the aid of your new yarn guide!

No pens around? No problem. Get a thick drinking straw. Cut it so you have a piece that is about 5 inches (12.5 cm) long. Thread your yarn through it and you are ready to start wrapping your yarn around the pegs.

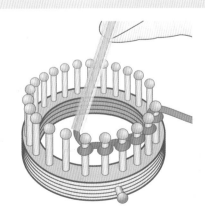

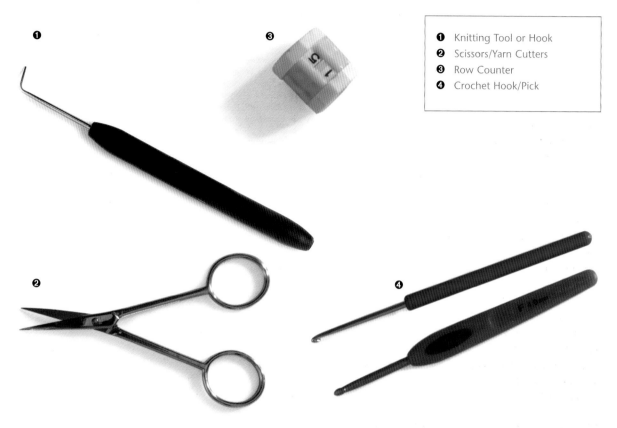

❶ Knitting Tool or Hook
❷ Scissors/Yarn Cutters
❸ Row Counter
❹ Crochet Hook/Pick

forget to change the setting. Row counters come in various shapes: cylindrical, square, and circular. There are two types of cylindrical-shaped row counter. One of them has an opening that is generally used to insert a knitting needle through; you can use it to fit over the knitting tool. The second one has a small ring attached to one of the sides that allows you to put it over a peg and keep it at the base of the knitting loom. The square and circular types are mechanical in that you only need to push a button to increase the numbers. Although all of them help in keeping track of rows, you have to remember to reset them at the beginning of each row.

Crochet Hooks are very useful. Don't worry—crochet knowledge is not necessary to loom knit, unless you want to crochet an edging around your knits. Crochet hooks just come in handy when picking up a dropped stitch or when binding off a flat panel from the knitting loom. It is advisable to have the size of crochet hook called for on the yarn label, as this will make it easier to handle the yarn. In general, carrying a medium-size hook in your accessories bag will suffice.

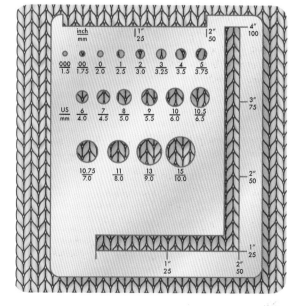

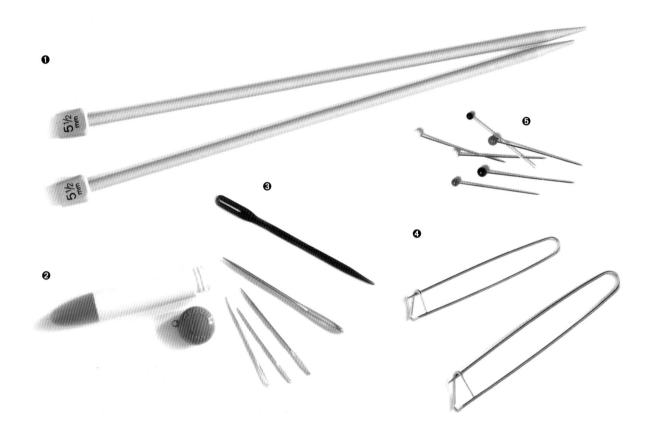

Single/Double-Pointed Knitting Needles

Don't run, wait! You won't be using them to knit. There, you can relax! The needles are only going to be used as stitch holders for grafting the toes of socks. I would recommend obtaining a pair of size 8 (5 mm) and a pair of size 2 (2.75 mm). The size 8 can be used with the large and regular gauge looms, while the size 2 can be used with the smaller gauges.

Tapestry Needles

Tapestry Needles are used for seaming the sides of a knitted garment, for gathering and closing the ends of hats, and for weaving in the ends on the knitted garment. Tapestry needles come in plastic and metal. They have a larger eye than regular sewing needles. The plastic needles are flexible and allow you to bend them. The metal needles are smoother and won't snag the knitted item. Both styles of needle have blunt ends that prevent the splitting of the yarn. As with the crochet hooks, the needles come in different sizes, and the eye opening can fit certain thicknesses of yarn; it is advisable to have a collection of needles that differ in the size of the eye opening.

Pins

Pins have uses everywhere in the knitting world; they can turn a curled piece of stockinette into a nice straight sleeve. Pins are essential tools in the finishing of knitted pieces. The straight pins with colored heads are perfect to use when seaming two sides together. Large T-pins make blocking a knitted garment a breeze. These pins can be found at any yarn shop. Do not use any other household pin as it may rust and leave rust spots on your knits.

Stitch Holders

Stitch Holders look like oversized safety pins, except they have a blunt end. They are useful for holding live stitches that will be worked on later in the project, like a neckline, or a tricky bit of shaping. They come in different sizes and it is advisable to have an array of sizes in your knitting bag. Small coil-less safety pins also come in handy when holding only a few stitches or marking the right or reverse side of the knitted item.

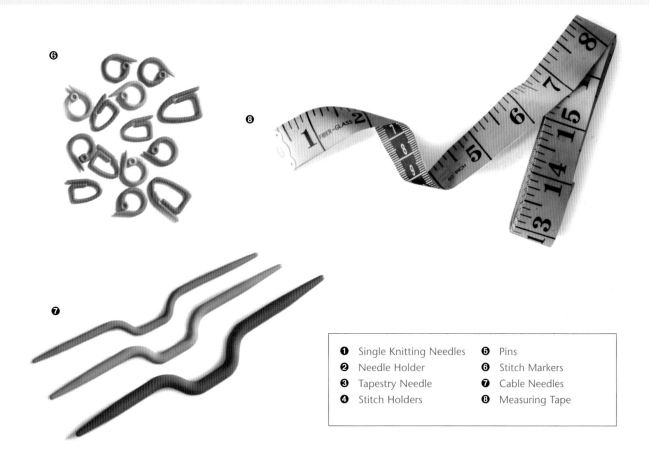

❶	Single Knitting Needles	❺	Pins
❷	Needle Holder	❻	Stitch Markers
❸	Tapestry Needle	❼	Cable Needles
❹	Stitch Holders	❽	Measuring Tape

Stitch Markers are small rings that can be used to mark the pegs where special stitches or treatments need to be done on the knitted item. Stitch markers are generally used on needles, but they fit perfectly over the pegs on a knitting loom, resting on the base, where they serve to remind the loomer that the peg has a stitch that requires special treatment.

Split ring stitch markers are very helpful in marking a stitch itself rather than the peg. The open split rings are removable by simply opening the ring and sliding it off the peg. They come in various shapes, sizes, and colors. It is best to have a variety of different colors.

Measuring Tape or Ruler is a loom knitter's best friend; no knitting bag should be without at least one. When choosing a good measuring tape, choose material that won't distort easily. Discard any measuring tape at the first sign of wear, even if it's your favorite. A distorted measuring tape can mean disaster to your knitted garment, as it won't measure accurately. It is also advisable to have a small plastic ruler on hand.

Cable Needles come in different shapes and sizes. They are available in plastic and metal. Usually, one package contains three different sizes; choose the size that best works with the yarn in the project. Until very recently, loom knitters were not able to create cables, as the nonelasticity of the stitches as set on the knitting loom made it difficult. However, this has now changed, and so cable needles have been added to the loomer's extensive gadget repertoire!

Calculator Yep, you read it right, we will still be doing math. I know you thought math was long gone with school, but it has come to haunt you again; math wants to be your best friend. No worries though—you can cheat this time and use a calculator. A calculator comes in very handy when calculating gauge or even adding a few pegs to the count in the pattern.

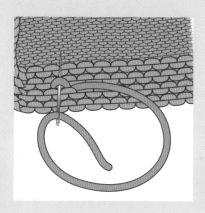

CHAPTER 2
Basic Techniques

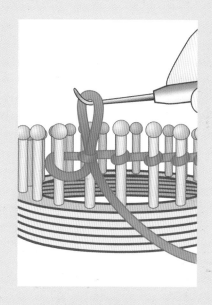

In this section, you will learn the basics of loom knitting as well as some techniques to help you complete the designs in this book.

Casting On

The foundation row for loom knits is called the cast-on row, abbreviated as CO. Every cast-on method starts with a slipknot.

Slipknot

1 Leaving a 5-inch (12.5-cm) beginning tail, form a circle with the working yarn (the one coming from the skein). Fold the circle over the working yarn.

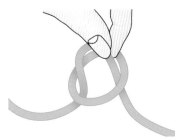

2 Reach through the circle, and grab the yarn coming from the skein.

3 Pull the working yarn through the circle, while also pulling gently on the short end of the yarn tail end, thus tightening the noose on the knot.

The e-wrap CO

This cast-on is called the e-wrap because if you look at it from above it resembles a cursive "e." It is the easiest method to learn. Use the e-wrap cast-on method when the first row needs to be picked up for a brim or seam, or when the cast-on row needs to be extremely flexible.

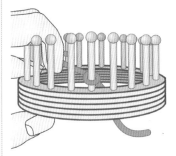

1 Place a stitch marker on any of the pegs on the knitting loom. The peg with the stitch marker will be your starting peg. Make a slipknot, and place it on the peg with the stitch marker.

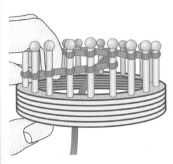

3 Wrap each peg a second time using the same method. Each peg should have two loops on it. Hold the working yarn in place so the wraps do not unravel.

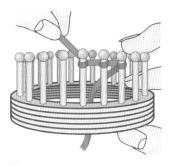

2 Holding the loom in front of you with the working yarn in your left hand, work around the knitting loom in a clockwise direction thus: * Pull the working yarn toward the inside of the loom, wrap around the peg directly to the left, in a counterclockwise direction around the peg. * Repeat from * to * with each of the pegs. Continue wrapping each peg in a counterclockwise direction, until you complete one round (each peg should have one loop). Notice how the yarn crosses over itself on the inside of the knitting loom.

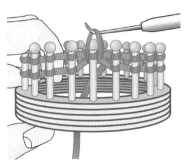

4 Insert the tip of the knitting tool into the bottommost loop on the last peg wrapped. Lift the loop up and off the peg and allow the loop to fall toward the inside of the knitting loom. The process of lifting the loops off the pegs is known as knitting over, abbreviated as ko. Go to the peg directly to the left and repeat this step, knitting over. Repeat all around the loom until each peg has only one wrap. Ready, set, go!

Long tail CO

This is known as the long tail cast-on because you use the tail of the yarn and the working yarn to create the cast-on. This term is also used in needle knitting. It creates a flexible cast-on.

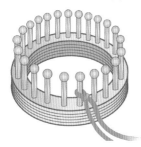

1 Make a slipknot, leaving a tail that is about four times as long as the width of your project. Place the slipknot on a peg. The slipknot will become your first stitch.

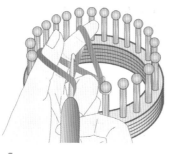

2 Position your left hand palm down: wrap the working yarn around your index finger and the tail over your thumb. Hold both yarn ends with the remaining three fingers.

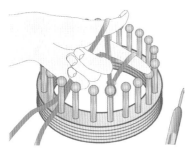

3 Flip your hand toward the left until your palm faces up. The hand is now in a slingshot position.

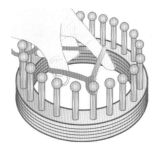

4 Guide a crochet hook by the palm side of the thumb under the yarn strand, then guide it over to the yarn strand on the index finger, hook the yarn strand on the index finger, and guide it down through the loop on your thumb.

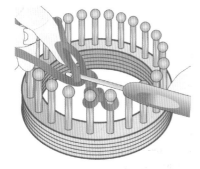

5 Place the loop on the adjacent empty peg. Remove your thumb from its loop and gently tug on the yarn tail to tighten the new stitch that you created.

Repeat steps 3–5 until you have the number of stitches called for in the pattern.

No Crochet Hook?

There is a method of using the long tail cast-on without a crochet hook but it is slightly more complicated.

1 With the slipknot on your first peg, grab the tail yarn and e-wrap the peg to the left. The peg now has two loops. Knit over so only one loop remains.

2 Grab yarn coming from the skein and e-wrap the next empty peg.

3 Grab the tail yarn and place it above the e-wrap done in step 2. Lift the bottom loop over and off the peg (the peg should remain wrapped with the tail).

4 Repeat steps 2 and 3 with the remaining pegs.

TIPS

● You may find it more comfortable to place the loom on your lap or a table to work on the cast-on.

● When making your slipknot, it is better to overestimate and make the tail too long rather than too short.

Basic Stitches

The two basic stitches are knit and purl. With these two stitches you will be able to create numerous stitch patterns for your loom knits. There are 3 different ways to work a Knit Stitch, see the side panel for the most appropriate for your project.

KNIT STITCH BASICS

Knit stitch: tall height and wider stitch
U-stitch: medium height and medium width
Flat stitch: short height and narrower width

Knit stitch (k)

The knit stitch is the cornerstone of any loom-knitted item. Known also as the plain stitch, it resembles the knit stitch created on knitting needles and looks like a small "V." **Preparation:** The knitting loom must have at least one stitch on each peg (a cast-on row).

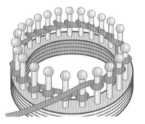 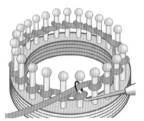 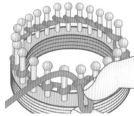 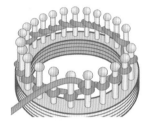

1 Lay the working yarn in front and above the stitch on the peg.

2 Insert the knitting tool through the stitch on the peg from bottom up. You will hook the working yarn where the red ring indicates.

3 Hook the working yarn with the knitting tool, making a loop. Grab the loop with your fingers.

4 Take the original loop off the peg and replace with the new. Tighten the working yarn. Repeat steps 1–4 to complete a row.

Flat stitch (fs)

This variation looks exactly like the knit stitch, except it is shorter and tighter.

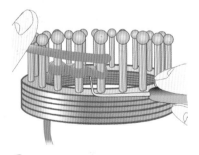 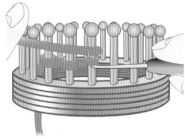 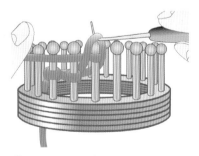

1 Take the working yarn to the front of the peg and place it above the loop on the peg. Do not place any tension on it; simply rest it above.

2 Insert the tool through the loop.

3 Lift the loop off the peg.

U-stitch (u-st)

This variation looks exactly like the knit stitch, except that it is shorter and tighter. However, it is a little bigger and not as tight as the flat stitch.

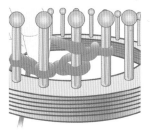 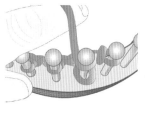 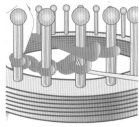 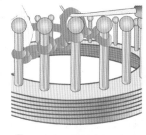

1 Take the working yarn to the front of the peg and place it above the loop on the peg.

2 Wrap the working yarn around the peg, as if hugging the peg with the yarn.

3 Insert the knitting tool through the loop on the peg.

4 Lift the loop off the peg.

Purl stitch (p)

The purl stitch is the reverse of a knit stitch and shows as a small horizontal bump on the front.

Preparation: The knitting loom must have at least one stitch on each peg (a cast-on row).

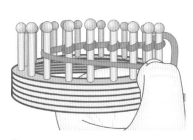 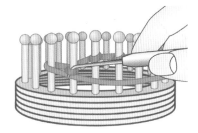 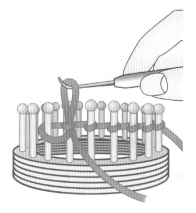

1 Lay the working yarn in front of and below the stitch on the peg.

2 Insert the knitting tool from top to bottom through the stitch on the peg and scoop up the working yarn with the knitting tool.

3 Pull the working yarn through the stitch on the peg to form a loop. Hold the new loop with your fingers.

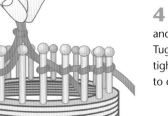

4 Take the old loop off the peg and place the new loop on the peg. Tug gently on the working yarn to tighten the stitch. Repeat steps 1–4 to complete a purl row.

Bringing up the cast-on row

This technique is used to create a picot edge or to create a brim/cuff on a hat.

Preparation: Work as many rows as indicated in pattern.

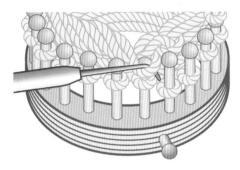

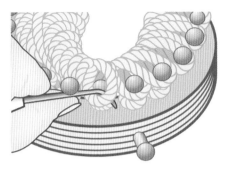

1 Reach inside the knitting loom, and find the beginning yarn tail end. Align the beginning yarn tail end with the first peg on the knitting loom. Next to the beginning tail end, locate the very first cast-on stitch. Place the stitch on the corresponding peg. Repeat this step with the remaining stitches. Each peg should have two loops on it.

2 Knit over by lifting the bottom loop off the peg. After all the stitches have been knitted over, the loom should only have one loop on each peg.

Binding Off

Although it is the last step in creating the projects, binding off is as important as any other part of the knitted item, and has an impact on how the final piece will look.

Basic bind-off

This creates a firm, crochet-like edge. It can be used at the end of a project to bind off all the stitches, as well as when you have to bind off only a certain number of stitches to make an opening.

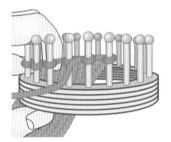

1 Knit two stitches (pegs 1 and 2).

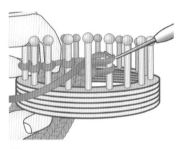

2 Move the loop from the second peg over to the first peg. Knit over.

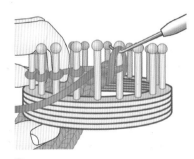

3 Move the loop on the first peg over to the peg just emptied.

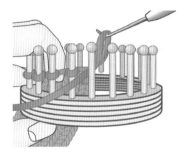

4 Knit the next peg. Repeat steps 2–4 until you have bound off the required number of stitches. A stitch will remain on the last peg. Cut the yarn leaving a long tail. E-wrap the peg, knit over, and pull the tail end through the stitch.

Yarn over bind-off

The yarn over bind-off provides a stretchy border, perfect for items that need flexible openings.

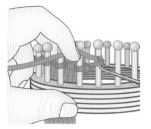

1 Knit the first stitch (peg 1).

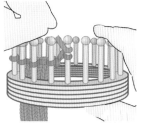

2 Wrap the peg in a clockwise direction.

3 Knit over and knit the next stitch (peg 2).

4 Move the loop from the second peg to the first. Knit over. Repeat steps 2–4 until one stitch remains. Cut the yarn leaving a tail. E-wrap the peg, knit over, and pull the tail end through.

Gather bind-off

The gather removal method allows you to finish a tube into a gathered end, perfect for socks. Knit the tube until you have reached the desired length.

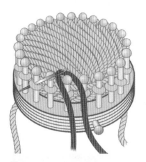

1 Cut the working yarn coming from the project, leaving a 5-inch (12.5-cm) tail. Or, if necessary, cut another piece of yarn that is at least twice the circumference of the knitting loom. Thread the gathering yarn through a tapestry needle.

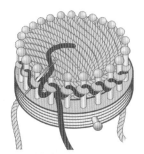

2 Go to the first peg, and pass the needle and yarn through the loop on the peg, leaving a 5-in (12.5-cm) tail. Go to the second peg and pass the needle and yarn through the loop on the peg. Continue around the loom until you reach the last peg. Pass the needle and thread through the first stitch once more.

3 Remove the loops off the pegs. Gently pull on the beginning and end tails of the gathering yarn. Continue pulling on the tail ends until the top of the item is closed. Use the tapestry needle to sew the hole closed.

4 Grab the yarn tail end coming from the knitting of the project. Tie the three strands (the two ends from the gathering yarn and the one from the knitting of the project) together. Make a square knot and weave in the ends.

Weaving in the Tail Ends

When you have finished your first project, it is almost ready to be used, but you still need to hide those unsightly tail ends from your yarn. What to do?

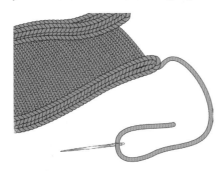 

1 Locate the yarn tail end and thread it through the large eye of a tapestry needle.

2 Working on the wrong side of the item weave the yarn tail end by inserting the needle through the "bump" of each knit stitch. Go along and back in one row for about an inch in each direction.

Working in the Round

Working in the round on a knitting loom is quite simple; just complete one round and then continue going around on the loom. The most important aspect is joining the cast-on row to form the circle. There are a few choices: simple join, crossover join, and tail-end join.

Simple join

Take the working yarn from the last peg over to the first peg and begin working your first round. There will be a small gap between the first and last peg, but you can close it with the tail end when you are done working on the project.

Crossover join

In this case, the loop from the first peg exchanges places with the loop from the last peg. You will need to carefully remove the stitch from the first peg and hold it. Place the loop from the last peg over on the first peg. Place the loop you are holding on the last peg.

Tail-end join

When working the first round, pick up the working yarn and the tail coming from the slipknot. Treat both yarns as one and work the first three stitches with both yarns. These three stitches will have the double yarn—remember to pick up both when working on these three pegs on the next round.

Flat Panel Knitting

Mastering flat panels on a knitting loom is essential as it opens up possibilities to many new projects beyond hats or tubular knits.

From A to B and back again...

Knitting a flat panel on the knitting loom is not much different from knitting circularly. You can follow the same cast-on methods, knit the same stitches, and use the same bind-off methods.

However, there are a few things that differ. Since you are not knitting circularly around the knitting loom, you will have a starting point and an ending point. At both ends you will have a turning peg/stitch marking the beginning of a new row or the end of the last one.

When starting at point A, the peg at point A is your beginning peg. The peg at point B becomes your last peg, and will also be your turning peg. When you finish a row, by knitting the peg at point B, you turn and knit back to point A. Thus the pegs at points A and B alternate as turning pegs and beginning and ending pegs for the rows.

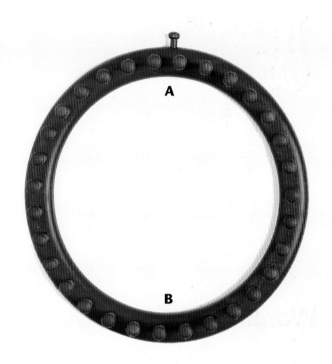

Beware of the selvedge

Now you are no longer going round in circles, you will have edges to deal with. The edge stitches of a knitted flat panel are called edge or selvedge stitches. When knitting from a pattern, look for instructions on how to treat the selvedge stitches. One way is to wrap the turning pegs and knit them. Alternatively you can slipstitch the first stitch on each row.

A slip stitch (sl st) is simply a stitch that is not knitted. You skip the peg, take the yarn to the next peg, and knit it. Using a slip stitch at the beginning of each row creates a chain-like edge at both sides of the knitted item.

How to decide which turning option to use? If you are going to be seaming two pieces together or adding a border, it is best to knit the edge stitches (always knit the first and last stitches). If you are looking for a more decorative edging, slip the first stitch of every row. However, slipping the stitch on each row will reduce the width of your knitted item by two stitches. If the pattern doesn't allow for this, you will have to add one stitch to either side of the pattern as you go along.

GLOSSARY

Selvedge As its name suggests, this is the self-made edge of the fabric you are creating, sometimes disappearing when you sew a seam, but sometimes a more visible finished edge.

Making I-Cords on a Loom

Cords can be made on spools, or any circular knitting loom that is small enough to be worked like a small spool knitter, or you can create I-cords by using a round loom as a rake.

3-Stitch I-cord

Notes:
- I-cord is knitted with the Knit Stitch.
- Work the loom in a clockwise direction (right to left).

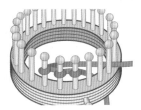

1 Cast on 3 pegs. With working yarn coming from the third peg run the yarn behind the pegs to the first peg.

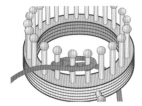

2 Bring yarn to the front of the loom and knit the 3 pegs.

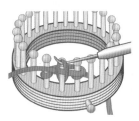

3 Knit the second peg, then the first, and the third last. Repeat until the cord measures the desired length.

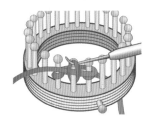

4 Bind off by cutting the yarn leaving a 4-inch (10 cm) tail. Move the loop from second to first peg. Knit over. Move the loop on peg 1 to peg 2. Move the loop on peg 3 to peg 2. Knit over. With working yarn, e-wrap peg 2. Knit over. Pull the last loop off the peg and pull on the yarn tail end.

Shaping

Learning the techniques of increasing and decreasing stitches within the knitted fabric allows us to add more details to our designs.

Smart shaping

As a new loom knitter, you may be tempted to simply cast on the desired number of additional stitches at the end of the row, but if you increase within the row, the knitted item will maintain its edge shaping. The increasing techniques described here are recommended whenever you need to increase one or two stitches within a row. Casting on is recommended when increasing more than two stitches on the edge of the row.

Increase (inc)

Adding extra stitches to the panel makes it wider. When increases happen within rows, it is advisable to only increase two stitches on a given row. Increases are used to shape sweater sleeves, skirts, and items that fan out. There are various ways to increase stitches on the loom, and all of them require you to move the stitches outwards to the empty pegs to allow room, or an empty peg, for the new stitch. Below are three methods for increasing familiarize yourself with all three.

Make 1 (M1)

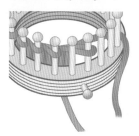

1 Move the last stitch to the next empty peg outwards, leaving an empty peg between the last two stitches.

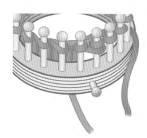

2 Knit the stitches on the knitting loom. When you reach the empty peg, e-wrap it and continue knitting to the end of the row. Increasing in this manner will leave a small hole where the increase was created.

Lifted Increase

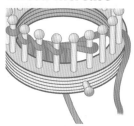

1 Move the last stitch outwards to the next empty peg, leaving an empty peg between the last two stitches.

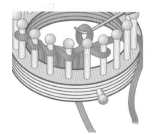

2 With the knitting tool reach for the ladder running from the two stitches on either side below the empty peg. Twist the strand and place it on the empty peg (if you don't twist it, you will create a small hole). Knit your row as usual.

Row Below

This is another way of increasing, using a crochet hook.

1 Move the last stitch to the next empty peg outwards, leaving an empty peg between the last two stitches. Get a crochet hook.
2 Knit to the empty peg, and with the crochet hook reach one stitch below (on the wrong side), pass the hook through one of the "legs" of the stitch and hook the working yarn, making a loop. Place the loop on the empty peg. Make sure not to pull on the stitch below too much as this may cause the stitch to pull together.

TIP

When creating a piece that will require many increases, make sure to cast on to a loom that is big enough to hold all the stitches you'll need.

Decrease (dec)

Removing stitches from your piece will make the piece narrower. When decreases happen within rows it is recommended to decrease one or two stitches in from either edge to keep the selvedge neat. There are various ways to decrease on the knitting loom; all of them require you to move the stitches inwards. Familiarize yourself with the methods below.

Knit 2 Together (k2tog)

Knitting 2 together creates a right-slanting decrease, and is best created at the beginning of a knit row.

Slip, Slip Knit (ssk)

The left-slanting decrease is the mirror image of a k2tog and is achieved by a slip, slip knit at the end of a row.

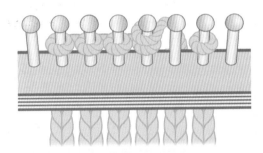

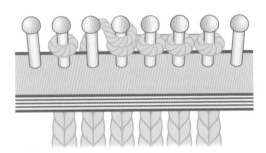

1 Move the stitch from peg 2 to peg 3 (the peg to its left). Peg 3 now has two stitches and peg 2 is empty. Note: the stitch from peg 3 will be on the bottom and the stitch from peg 2 is on top. When knitting over, the stitch that was on peg 2 will disappear behind the stitch from peg 3.

2 Move stitches inwards so there are no empty pegs. Knit the row as usual, making sure to knit 2 over 1 on the peg with the extra stitch.

1 Move the stitch from peg 2 over to peg 3 (or the peg to its right). Note: The stitch from the right peg (peg 3) is on the bottom, the stitch from the left peg (peg 2) is on top. Do not change the order of the loops—keep the bottom loop on the bottom and the top on the top.

2 Move stitches inwards so there are no empty pegs. Continue knitting as usual down the row.

Purl 2 together (p2tog)

This is a right-slanting decrease, best created at the beginning of a purl side row. It is made just like the k2tog above, except in a purl row.

1 Purl the row as usual. When you reach the peg with the extra stitch, lay the yarn below the two loops, and purl them, making sure to remove the two loops off the peg and leaving the newly formed loop.

> **TIP**
>
> It is best to do all increases/decreases at least one or two stitches away from the edge. Creating the increases/decreases right on the edge can cause sloppy edges and it makes picking up stitches very difficult.

Increasing two stitches or more

In certain instances, a pattern will call for increasing more than two stitches at any given row. In this case, it is best to cast on the stitches using the e-wrap cast on method (see pg. 26).

1 Knit the entire row as called for in the pattern. With the working yarn coming from the last stitch, cast on to the empty pegs using the chain cast-on method. When you reach the desired peg number, stop.

2 The loom is threaded with the extra stitches and is now ready. Turn back and knit or purl these stitches as directed by the pattern.

Decreasing two stitches or more

A pattern sometimes will ask you to bind off stitches at a certain point within the pattern.

1 Knit to the stitch where the binding off is supposed to begin.

2 Start bind-off using the basic bind-off method (see page 30). Stop when you have bound off the number of stitches called for in the pattern.

Most patterns will let you know which increase or decrease method you should use. If there is no information about which method to use, knit a small swatch and experiment with the different methods above to see which one looks best. The increases on a sleeve, for example, usually come in pairs—k2tog at the beginning of the row and ssk at the end. Look for these mirror images whenever you are knitting something that has increases or decreases at each end.

Short-row shaping

The short row shaping technique allows you to shape a knitted piece without decreasing stitches. It creates soft curves by knitting a row to a certain stitch in the row, then turning back and knitting in the other direction. It is commonly used in heels, and in any other item where you want seamless curves. Shaping with short rows has one pitfall that you must be aware of: it is necessary to "wrap" the stitch after the turning point to avoid a hole between the turning stitch and the next stitch. The "wrap" eliminates this hole almost completely (see below).

How to wrap and turn (W&T)

When knitting each wrapped peg, lift both the wrap and the stitch together, 2 over 1, as this will eliminate the wrap and fill the hole made with the short rows.

1 Knit or purl to the desired turning stitch. Take the stitch off the next peg and hold it with your knitting tool.

2 Wrap the peg by taking the yarn towards the inside of the loom and wrapping around the peg. The working yarn will end up to the front of the knitting loom.

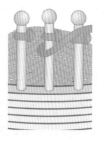

3 Place the stitch back on the peg. Take the working yarn and knit or purl back across the row.

Cables

A cable is a design feature that creates a rope-like twist in the knitting.

A cable twist is created by placing a few stitches on hold on a cable needle, so that they may be worked out of their usual order. Although cables may seem a bit intimidating at first, with practice you will find that they are quite simple.

Cables work best when created with yarns that have some inherent elasticity—for instance yarns with wool content. Use a cable needle or a double-pointed knitting needle to hold your stitches while you cross them.

When creating a cable, the stitches on the right side of the loom (when the loom is facing you) are held on the

cable needle (without being worked) while you work on the stitches to the left. Depending on the type of lean you want on your cable, you will hold the cable needle either toward the center of the loom or toward the front of the loom. If the cable needle is held in front of the work, the cable will twist to the left. This is the **left cross** (LC), also known as **front cross** (FC). If the cable needle is held to the center of the loom (back of work) the cable will have a right twist. This is the **right cross** (RC), also known as the **back cross** (BC).

Left cross (LC)—2 stitches

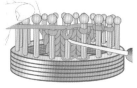

1 Take working yarn behind peg 1 (you are skipping peg 1).

2 Knit peg 2 and place stitch on cable needle and hold it to the center of the loom.

3 Move stitch from peg 1 to peg 2 (leaving peg 1 empty).

4 Place stitch from cable needle on peg 1.

5 Knit peg 2.

Right cross (RC)—2 stitches

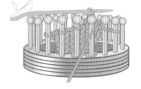

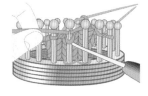

1 Place stitch from peg 1 on cable needle and hold to the center of the knitting loom.

2 Take working yarn in front of peg 2 and knit peg 2.

3 Move stitch from peg 2 to peg 1.

4 Place stitch from cable needle on peg 2.

5 Knit peg 2.

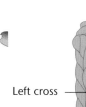

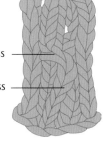

Left cross ———

Right cross ———

Left cross (LC)— 3 stitches

1 Take working yarn behind pegs 1 and 2 (skipping pegs 1 and 2).

2 Knit peg 3. Place stitch from peg 3 onto cable needle.

3 Knit peg 1 and peg 2. Move them over to pegs 2 and 3 as follows: stitch from peg 2 to peg 3, stitch from peg 1 to peg 2.

4 Place stitch from cable needle onto peg 1.

Right cross (RC)—3 stitches

1 Place stitch from peg 1 on cable needle and hold to center of knitting loom.

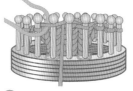

2 Knit peg 2 and peg 3.

3 Move the stitches from pegs 2 and 3 to pegs 1 and 2.

4 Place the stitch from cable needle on peg 3. Knit peg 3.

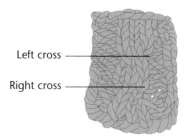

Left cross

Right cross

Left cross (LC)—4 stitches

1 Remove stitches from pegs 1 and 2 and place them on cable needle.
2 Knit pegs 3 and 4. Transfer stitches to pegs as follows: Stitch from peg 3 to peg 1; stitch from peg 4 to peg 2.
3 Transfer the stitches from cable needle to emptied pegs 3 and 4. Knit these 2 stitches.
4 Go to each of the loops on pegs 1–4 and gently pull out any yarn slack so it tightens the cable.

Right cross (RC)—4 stitches

1 Take working yarn behind pegs 1 and 2 (you are skipping pegs 1 and 2).
2 Knit peg 3 and 4. Place loops from pegs 3 and 4 on cable needle.
3 Knit pegs 1 and 2. Move them over as follows: stitch from peg 2 to peg 4; stitch from peg 1 to peg 3.
4 Take the stitches off the cable needle and place them on pegs 1 and 2.
5 Go to each of the stitches on pegs 1–4 and gently pull out any yarn slack so it tightens the cable.

Purl cables with 2 stitches

Achieving left cross purl (LCP) and right cross purl (RCP) cables is easy.
LCP: Follow the left cross (LC) instructions, except in step 2, purl instead of knit peg 2.
RCP: Follow the right cross (RC) instructions, except in step 5, purl instead of knit peg 2.

Purl cables with 3 stitches

To achieve left cross purl (LCP) and right cross purl (RCP) with 3 and 4 stitches, the crossing stitches are purled rather than knitted.
LCP: At step 2, purl instead of knit peg 3.
RCP: At step 4, purl instead of knit peg 3.

Working with Color

Adding color to your knits is a great way to liven up your projects. Below are various ways that you can use to spice up your knits.

Stripes

Creating stripes is the easiest way of spicing up a project. Knitting stripes allows you to use as many colors as you wish without having to carry more than one color at a time within the row. Gather all your odd skeins and try wide stripes, narrow stripes, or mixing wild colors and textured yarns. Your one-of-a-kind creation will have one main color (MC) with one (or more) contrasting colors (CC). When more than one contrasting color is used, the colors are designated by letters, such as A, B, C, D, and so on.

Horizontal stripes

Knit a few rows with your main color. When it's time to change to a new color, join the new yarn at the beginning of a row. After you have your desired colors set up, you can carry the various yarns along the edge of the item if you are knitting thin stripes. If you are knitting wider stripes, cut the yarn at the end of a row, and join yarns at the beginning of a row.

Vertical stripes

Creating thin vertical stripes is simple. You don't have to weave the yarns at the back of the work; the unused yarn can be carried behind the work. You will need yarn in two colors: a main color (MC) and a contrasting color (CC).

1 Pick up the MC and knit the stitches you desire in the main color, skip the ones you desire in contrasting color.
2 Go back to the beginning of the row, pick up the CC and knit all the pegs skipped in step 1.
3 Repeat steps 1–2 throughout.

TIP

Jogless stripes

1 Knit the first round with contrasting color: work normally.
2 Knit the second round with CC: skip the first stitch with yarn to the back of the stitch, work the rest of the stitches as indicated on the pattern.
3 Consecutive rounds are with CC: work normally.
4 Repeat above steps when creating more stripes.

Fair Isle

Fair Isle is a multicolored knitting technique, where a row is worked with only two colors in small repeating sections of patterns. Traditional Fair Isle knitting is worked completely in stockinette stitch and the items are usually circular. The circular nature of the item helps to hide the floats created by the color changes within the row. When carrying the unused color, it is recommended not to carry it over more than 5–7 stitches, or 1–1½ inches (2.5–4 cm).
Fair Isle patterns are usually depicted in chart form and share some characteristics with regular knitting charts. Each square represents a stitch. The squares will either be colored in or will have a color symbol and key. For circular knitting, you read the chart starting at the bottom, right side. Continue reading the next rounds starting at the right side.
Although it may seem complicated, the process of painting with your yarn is quite simple. There are two methods that you can use:

Method 1: This keeps your yarns separated and untangled. You pick up the main color at the beginning of a row, knit the required stitches and then drop it at the end of the row. Pick up the contrasting color and knit all the required stitches with that color, then drop it.

Method 2: You carry both yarns with you in your dominant hand as you work the stitch pattern. When the pattern calls for the CC, drop the MC color, bring the CC above the MC working yarn and knit as required. When the pattern calls for the MC, drop the CC and reach below for the MC color. Every time you change yarns, drop the one above and then reach below for the other.

Weave the two colors around each other at the back of the work to prevent holes showing

To weave the yarns around each other: knit a few stitches with the MC color, drop it and pick up the CC, wrap the CC around the MC, drop the CC, pick up the MC and keep on knitting. Take both colors to the back of the work, and twist them together.

Needle Felting

Needle Felting is a great way to add accents to your felted knits. It's achieved by poking natural fibers into a piece of felted fabric. The needles used for felting are special needles that have small sharp barbs that help lock the dry fibers onto the felted fabric. When the needle is poked or pushed into the felted fabric, the barbs pull the fiber down locking the fibers together. In addition to the needles, a piece of thick foam is used to place under the felted fabric to protect the user from accidental needle harm. The materials you will need to get started are the following:

1 Felted fabric
2 Needle felting kit—visit your local knitting store to obtain one. The needle felting kit comes with a thick foam and a set of standard beginner barbed needles.
3 Dyed roving, wool yarn or other natural fiber.
4 A needle felting design.

When you have your materials together, decide where you want to place the needle felting design on the felted fabric. Place the foam under the area where you want the needle felting design, choose your fiber/yarn and begin poking with the barbed needle. Continue utilizing the barbed needle until the design achieves the desired appearance. Add or remove fibers from the felted fabric as desired. If a mistake is made, remove the yarn out with your fingers and start again. The fibers come out easily, however, they stay in place unless purposely pulled out. Caution, be sure to move the foam piece as you move your design, you need to place it directly under your working area at all times to protect the user from accidental needle harm.

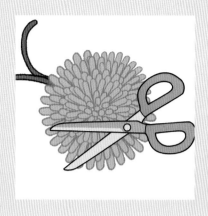

CHAPTER 3
Finishing Touches

Using the correct sewing-up technique is essential to creating the right look for your project, and this chapter explains it all. Plus all the embellishment techniques needed for a perfect finish.

Finishing Touches

Here we look at the different types of stitches you might use in your sewing up, to give you all you need to make the best job of finishing up your beautiful projects.

Mattress stitch

1 Lay the pieces to be joined, right side up and side-by-side. Thread a tapestry needle with the tail end. Bring the yarn through to the front, in the middle of the first stitch on the first row of the seam. Take the needle through to the same position on the other piece, and bring it out in the middle of the edge stitch one row up.

2 Insert the needle back into the first piece of fabric, in the same place that the yarn last came out. Then bring the needle out in the middle of the stitch above. Repeat this, making a zigzag seam from edge to edge for a few more rows. You can pull the thread firmly, and the stitches almost disappear. When the seam is finished, weave in the ends.

Grafting

Also known as the Kitchener stitch, grafting allows you to join two panels of knitted fabric invisibly. The process is simple, although at first it may seem daunting. Just take it step-by-step and you will be on your way to invisible seams. In the case of socks, the toe area is grafted to the instep of the sock.

When you are preparing for grafting, you need to mount the stitches correctly on the needle. Correct position ensures proper grafting. Imagine the following: the knit stitch consists of two arms: a right and a left arm. While holding the needle on the left hand, the stitches should sit on the needle with the right arm toward the front of the work.

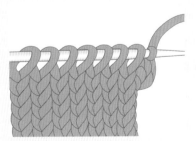

The stitches should sit like the illustration above.

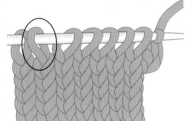

Incorrect mounting: note how the left arm toward the front of the needle faces left..

Preparation

1 Cut working yarn coming from the sock, leaving a 3-yard (3-m) tail.
2 Transfer half of the stitches from the loom onto one double-pointed needle (in this example, loops from pegs 1 through 12).
3 Transfer the remaining half of the stitches to a second double-pointed needle (in this example, loops from pegs 13 through 24).
4 Thread a tapestry needle with the 3-yard (3-m) tail.

Working

For illustration purposes, a contrasting color yarn is used for the grafting row.

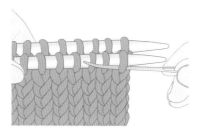

1 Hold knitting needles parallel to each other, wrong sides of the knitting together. Insert the tip of the tapestry needle through the first stitch on the front needle as if you were going to purl.

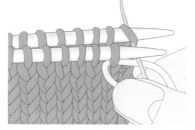

2 Insert yarn through the first stitch on the back needle as if to knit, pull the yarn through, but leave stitch on the knitting needle.

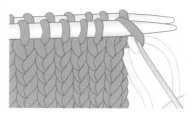

3 Insert the tip of the tapestry needle through the first stitch on the front needle as if you were going to knit, pull the yarn through the stitch, and slide that same stitch off the needle.

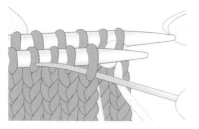

4 Insert the yarn needle through the next stitch on the front needle as if to purl, pull the yarn through, and leave the stitch on the needle.

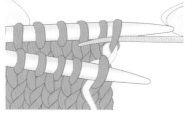

5 Bring the yarn to the side of the fabric (not over the needles) and insert the tapestry needle through the first stitch on the back needle as if to purl, bring the yarn through, and slide the stitch off the needle.

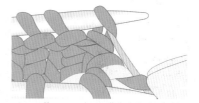

6 Insert the tapestry needle through the next stitch on the back needle as if to knit, pull the yarn through, and leave the stitch on the needle.

7 Repeat steps 3–6 across the row of stitches until only one stitch remains. Insert the tapestry needle through that last stitch and weave in ends.

TIP

If there are any uneven stitches, use the tapestry needle to gently tug on the little legs of the adjacent stitch until the stitches look even throughout the row.

Embellishing your Work

As well as color work, you can make each design your very own by adding different decorative elements, such as pom-poms, beading, fringes, tassels, embroidery, and special stitching.

Beads

Including beads in your work can make an ordinary project extraordinary! Do not be afraid to add them to your projects; the process is simple and it provides beautiful results.

Preparation: Before you can begin working with beads, you need to thread them onto the yarn.
1 Using a sewing needle and nylon thread, slide all the beads onto the thread.
2 Tie the end of the thread to the beginning of the yarn and slide all the beads down onto the yarn. Once all the beads are on the yarn, cut the nylon thread. You can now begin working.

Placing the beads
1 Take the working yarn to the front of the peg where you want the bead located.
2 Slide the bead down as closely as possible to the front of the peg.
3 Take the stitch off the peg and hold it.
4 With the knitting tool, lift the bead from step 2 and place it behind the peg.
5 Place the stitch back on the peg and take the working yarn to the front of the loom.
6 Work the next peg as indicated in the pattern.

Sequins

You can add sequins to your knits easily by using the beading method. Simply make sure that the sequins lie flat against the right side of the knitted fabric. You can also combine sequins and beads.
1 Place a small bead in the center of the sequin. Thread a very slim sewing needle with thread—any color of your choice.
2 Secure the thread on the wrong side of the fabric, bring the needle up where desired, thread on a sequin and then a small bead. Poke the needle back down through the center of the sequin.
3 Repeat the stitching through the bead at least one more time. Secure the thread in the wrong side by making a square knot.

Pompoms

Pompoms can add a fun factor to almost all projects. You can buy a little pompom gadget or you can make your own.

1 Cut two cardboard circles—the circle size will correspond to the pompom size. Make a small circular hole in each center. Cut about ¼ of each circle out, leaving you with a ¾ doughnut.

2 Place a piece of yarn in the center of the two doughnuts. Holding the doughnuts together, wrap the working yarn around the outer rims until the hole is full. The more yarn you wrap, the fluffier the pompom.

3 Using scissors, cut around the outside edge between the cardboard doughnuts. Tightly secure the pompom with the piece of yarn you placed at the center of the doughnuts.

4 Remove the cardboard. Fluff and shape the pompom. Trim any excess yarn to make ends uniform.

Tassels

Tassels are a decorative element made of strands of yarn tied at one end, typically seen at the corners of blankets.

Fringes

Fringes are a decorative element made out of strands of yarn. They are made of a set of tassels, but do not have a top yarn to secure them to the knitted fabric. Instead they are drawn securely through the edge of the knitted fabric.

1 You need two pieces of cardboard—the height of the cardboard corresponds to the length of the tassel. Sandwich a piece of yarn between the two pieces of cardboard. This is used later on to secure the top end of the tassel.

2 To make the tassel, wind yarn around the cardboard; the more wraps around the cardboard the bushier the tassel. Using the yarn sandwiched between the pieces of cardboard, secure the top of the tassel. Cut the strands at the bottom edge, along the cardboard. Remove the cardboard pieces.

1 Follow steps 1 and 2 from the Tassels instructions. Insert a crochet hook from front to back (or back to front) into the fabric's edge and pull the folded loop through the fabric.

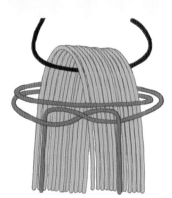

3 Wrap another length of yarn around the group of strands, about 1 inch (2.5 cm) below the top—5–10 wraps are recommended. Use the same color, or a contrasting color for extra effect. Hide the ends of the yarn inside the tassel. Trim the tassel ends to look uniform.

4 Use the free ends at the top of the tassel to secure it to the knitted project.

2 Bring the ends through the loop and secure the tassel by tightening. Once all the fringe has been attached to the knitted fabric, trim the strands of yarn to the same length for a uniform look.

Embroidery

Embroidery for me brings back memories of elementary school and a stern teacher telling me that my stem stitches needed a little more work in the straightness department. I remember being happy with the overall project, a panel that I gifted my grandmother for her tortillas warmer. Now, I add embroidery to all sorts of knitted fabric. I enjoy putting little lazy daisies on children's projects and creating little trees on cushions and afghans. You can add embroidery details to any stockinette background to make your project individual.

Embroidery guidelines

- Use a sharp needle with a large eye.
- Choose a smooth yarn, preferably the same fiber weight as the knitted project, or a little lighter weight.
- Pre-cut the yarn lengths about 24 inches (60 cm) or shorter.
- Always leave a 5–6 inch (12.5–15 cm) tail, to be used later to weave in the ends.
- When embroidering, keep a loose tension; embroidering too tightly can distort the knitted fabric.
- When complete, weave in all the tail ends through the wrong side, preferably behind the embroidered stitches.

Chain stitch

This stitch is used to create straight or curved lines and outlines.

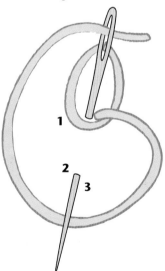

1 Bring the needle up at 1, form a loop with the thread, and insert the needle again at 1.

2 Bring it up at 2, inside formed loop, and pull through.

3 Make another loop by inserting the needle again through 2 and bring it out at 3. Repeat as required.

4 Lastly, make a tiny little stitch to secure the chain stitch in place.

Single chain stitch

The single chain stitch is sometimes called the lazy daisy stitch, and is often used to create small flower petals and small leaves.

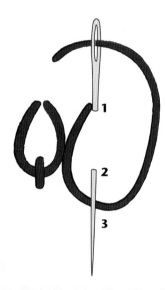

1 Bring the needle up at 1, forming a little loop with the thread. Insert needle at 1 once again.

2 Bring the needle back up at 2, inside the loop formed in step 1. Pull gently.

3 Insert needle at 3, catching the loop of thread.

Stem stitch

Stem stitch makes a slender line of stitches. I call it the skinny stitch, as it helps me remember the difference between it and the single chain stitch, which has more of a curvaceous body.

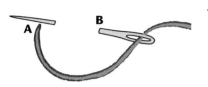

1 Bring the needle up at A and insert it back down at B.

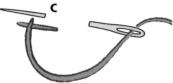

2 Bring the needle back up at C (midway and above A and B) and pull through.

3 Bring it back down at D. Repeat steps 2 and 3, moving towards the right.

French knots

I love to use French knots for flower centers and to embroider little eyes on knitted animals.

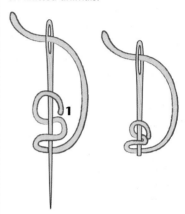

1 Bring the needle up at 1. Wind the thread twice around the needle tip.

2 Holding the thread with fingertips, insert needle as close to 1 as possible, and pull gently.

Duplicate stitch

Duplicate stitch is a decorative element used to embroider a design over the knitted stitches on the fabric. You will need a tapestry needle, yarn in contrasting color that is the same weight as the one of the knitted fabric, and an erasable fabric pen.

1 Using the erasable pen, color over the stitches that you want to embroider on.

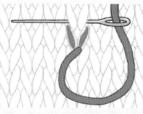

2 Thread the tapestry needle with contrasting color and insert it from the back of the work to the front through the bottom of the "V" of the stitch. Leave a 5-in (12.5-cm) tail in the back to weave in ends Thread the needle across the stitch above the one you are duplicating.

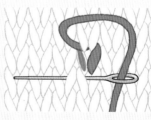

3 Insert the needle back into the bottom of the "V" (the same place as step 1). One stitch duplicated! Repeat with the other stitches that you need duplicated, until your motif is complete.
To duplicate vertically adjacent stitches: Sew under both the original stitch and the duplicate stitch.

CHAPTER 4
Scarves, Wraps, and Shrugs

Flat Panel Scarves for the Whole Family

The purls break the monotony of stockinette stitch for a more challenging knit. Ribbing provides a perfect fit every time!

MATERIALS

Knitting loom

Regular gauge knitting loom with at least 24 (44) pegs. Samples were knit using a blue Knifty Knitter long loom.

Yarn

4 250 yards (229 m) worsted weight yarn.
Male sample: Berroco Pure Merino wool, 100% extra fine merino wool, in Black and Storm, 92 yds (85 m) per 1.75 oz (50 g).
Female sample: Kollage Delightful, 68% Kid Mohair, 22% Viscose, 10% Polyester, in Mermaid, 100 yds (91 m) per 1.8 oz (53 g).
Child sample: Malabrigo Chunky, 100% merino wool, in Apple Green, Bobby Blue, Fuchsia, and Sauterne, 104 yds (95 m) per 3.5 oz (99.2 g).

Tools

Tapestry needle
Knitting tool

Gauge

8 sts x 12 rows = 2 in (5 cm) in rib stitch (stretched out)

Pattern note
Use a single strand throughout.

Stitch pattern
Rib Stitch Pattern:
Row 1: k1, *p2, k2; rep from * to last 3 sts, p2, k1.
Row 2: p1, *p2, k2; rep from * to last 3 sts, p2, p1.

Directions
BLACK AND GRAY SCARF
Using color A, cast on 44 stitches. Work rows 1–2 until item measures 8 inches (20 cm) from the cast-on edge. Join color B.
Continue in Rib Stitch Pattern, using B, until item measures 8 in (20 cm) less than desired length. Join A.
Continue in Rib Stitch Pattern until item measures 8 in (20 cm) from last color change.
Bind off with basic bind-off method. Weave ends in. Block lightly.

GREEN SCARF
Using C, cast on 24 stitches. Work rows 1–2 until item measures 62 in (157 cm), or desired length. Bind off with basic bind-off method. Weave ends in. Block lightly. Attach fringes to both ends of the scarf.

COLORFUL POMPOM SCARF
Using the Fuchsia color, cast on 24 stitches.
Work rows 1–2 until item measures 62 in (157 cm), or desired length. Change colors as follows:
8 rows – Fuchsia,
8 rows – Apple Green,
8 rows – Bobby Blue,
6 rows – Fuchsia,
6 rows – Sauterne,
4 rows – Apple Green,
8 rows – Fuchsia,
4 rows – Sauterne.
Bind off with basic bind-off method. Weave ends in. Block lightly.

Pompoms
Using all 4 colors, make 2 full pompoms.

Assembly
Fold the ends of the scarf to form a triangle shape. Sew the edges together to hold the triangle in place. Secure a pom-pom at the tip of each triangle.

Adamaris Shawl

Loom knitted as a flat panel, this shawl is wider than a regular scarf. The lace stitch pattern will keep both new loom knitters and seasoned loom knitters enthralled.

MATERIALS

Knitting loom

55-peg regular gauge knitting loom. Sample was knit using a Blue Knifty Knitter Long Loom.

Yarn

(3) 360 yards (330 m) light worsted weight yarn. [Louet KidLin, 53% kid mohair, 24% linen, 23% nylon, 120 yds (109 m) per 1.7 oz (50 g), was used in sample]

Tools

Stitch markers
Tapestry needle
Knitting tool

Gauge

7.5 sts x 11 rows = 2 in (5 cm)

Size

18 x 62 in (46 x 157 cm) blocked

Pattern note

Worked as a flat panel. Use a single strand throughout.

Stitch pattern
Chevron Stitch Pattern:

Row 1: *k2tog, yo, k1, yo, sl1—k1—psso, k2; rep from * to the end (see side panel).

Rows 2 & 4: Knit.

Row 3: *k2tog, yo, k3, yo, sl1—k1—psso; rep from * to the last st, k1 (see side panel).

Directions

Cast on 55 stitches.

First: Purl.

**Next row: k4, work row 1 of Chevron Stitch Pattern until last 2 sts, k2.

Next row: p2, work row 2 of Chevron Stitch Pattern until last 2 sts, p2.

Next row: k3, work row 3 of Chevron Stitch Pattern until last 3 sts, k3.

Next row: p2, work row 4 of Chevron Stitch Pattern until last 2 sts, p2.**

Repeat from ** to ** until item measures 60 inches (152 cm) in length, or the desired length.

Next row: Purl.
Bind off with basic bind-off method. Weave in ends and wet block to dimensions.

Symbol	Meaning
	Knit
●	Purl
O	YO
⋏	sl1-k1-psso
⁄	k2tog

55	54	53	52	51	50	49	48	47	46	45	44	43	42	41	40	39	38	37	36	35	34	33	32	31	30	29	28	27	26	25	24	23	22	21	20	19	18	17	16	15	14	13	12	11	10	9	8	7	6	5	4	3	2	1	
●	●																																																			●	●		4
		⋏	O			O	⁄	⋏	O			O	⁄	⋏	O			O	⁄	⋏	O			O	⁄	⋏	O			O	⁄	⋏	O			O	⁄	⋏	O			O	⁄	⋏	O					O	⁄				3
●	●																																																	●	●		2
		⋏	O	O	⁄		⋏	O	O	⁄		⋏	O	O	⁄		⋏	O	O	⁄		⋏	O	O	⁄		⋏	O	O	⁄		⋏	O	O	⁄		⋏	O	O	⁄		⋏	O	O	⁄								1

CHEVRON STITCH PATTERN
ROWS 1 AND 3

Row 1: *k2tog, yo, k1, yo, sl1—k1—psso, k2; rep from *to end.

* Step 1 Move loop from peg 1 to 2. Treating both loops on peg as one, knit peg 2.

Step 2 Move loop, peg 2 to 1.

Step 3 E-wrap peg 2.

Step 4 Knit peg 3.

Step 5 Lift loop from peg 4 and hold it.

Step 6 E-wrap peg 4. Place loop from step 5 back on peg.

Step 7 Knit peg 5.

Step 8 Move loop, peg 5 to 4.

Step 9 On peg 4, lift middle loop over and off the peg. (Peg is left with the e-wrap at the bottom and extra loop on top.)

Step 10 Move the top loop from peg 4 over to peg 5.

Step 11 Knit pegs 6 and 7. Rep from * to the end.

Row 3: *k2tog, yo, k3, yo, sl1—k1—psso; rep from * to the last st, k1.

Step 1 Move loop from peg 1 to 2. Treating both loops on the peg as one, knit peg 2.

Step 2 Move loop, peg 2 to 1.

Step 3 E-wrap peg 2.

Step 4 Knit peg 3, 4, 5.

Step 5 Lift loop from peg 6 and hold it.

Step 6 E-wrap peg 6. Place loop from Step 5 back on peg.

Step 7 Knit peg 7.

Step 8 Move loop from peg 7 to peg 6.

Step 9 On peg 6, lift middle loop over and off the peg. (Peg is left with the e-wrap at the bottom and extra loop on top.)

Step 10 Move the top loop from peg 6 over to peg 7. Rep from * to the end. from peg 6 over to peg 7. Rep from * to the end.

Symphony Lace Cowl

A shoulder wrap, a scarf, a cowl, all three in one! Loom knitted in a beaded lace weight yarn and a delightful lace stitch pattern makes for a beautiful drape garment.

MATERIALS

Knitting loom

56-peg regular gauge knitting loom. Sample was knit using a yellow Knifty Knitter long loom.

Yarn

1 300 yards (274 m) lace weight yarn. [Symphony Lace, 63% kid mohair, 10% silk, 18% nylon, 8% wool, in GoldenRod, 345 yds (315 m) per 2.8 oz (80 g), was used in sample]

Tools

Tapestry needle
Knitting tool
6 stitch markers—preferably
3 sets of different colors

Gauge

6 sts x 8 rows = 2 in (5 cm) blocked

Pattern notes

Use a single strand throughout. Work loosely for this project.

Feather & Fan Stitch Pattern

—multiple of 18 + 2
Row 1: Knit.
Row 2: Knit.
Row 3: k1, *[k2tog] 3 times, [yo, k1] 6 times, [k2tog] 3 times; rep from * to last st, k1 (see side panel).
Row 4: Purl.

BREAKDOWN OF SECTION FROM *, OVER 18 STITCHES

k1, *[k2tog] 3 times, [yo, k1] 6 times, [k2tog] 3 times

Step 1 Lift loop from peg 1 and hold it. Move loop from peg 2 and place on peg 1. Place the loop you are holding on peg 1. Peg 1 now has 2 loops on it.
Step 2 Lift loop from peg 3 and hold it. Move loop from peg 4 and place on peg 2. Place the loop you are holding on peg 2. Peg 2 has 2 loops on it.
Step 3 Lift loop from peg 5 and hold it. Move loop from peg 6 and place on peg 3. Place the loop you are holding on peg 3. Peg 3 has 2 loops on it.
Step 4 Move loop from peg 7 to peg 5.
Step 5 Move loop from peg 8 to peg 7.
Step 6 Move loop from peg 17 to peg 18.
Step 7 Move loop from peg 16 to peg 17. Move loop from peg

15 to peg 17.
Step 8 Move loop from peg 14 to peg 16. Move loop from peg 13 to peg 16.
Step 9 Move loop from peg 12 to peg 15.
Step 10 Move loop from peg 11 to peg 13.
Step 11 Move loop from peg 10 to peg 11.
Over the 18 pegs, the loom should look as follows:
Pegs 1, 2, & 3 have two loops on each of them.
Peg 4, 6, 8, 10, 12, & 14 are empty.
Pegs 5, 7, 9, 11, 13, & 14 have one loop.
Pegs 16, 17, & 18 have two loops on them.
Step 12: Knit the row, treat the pegs with two loops as one loop (k2tog), e-wrap the empty pegs to create the yarn overs (yo).

Directions

It is recommended that stitch markers be placed on pegs 1 and 18; 19 and 26; and 37 and 55 for ease in working row 3 of the stitch pattern.
Cast on 56 stitches.
Work Feather & Fan Stitch Pattern until panel measures 40 in (102 cm).
Bind off loosely with basic bind-off method.
Weave in ends and steam block.

Assembly

Fold the panel in half; flip the top half over to form a twist at the midpoint. Using mattress stitch, sew the cast-on edge and bind-off edge together.
Wear as a cowl or as a shawl across the shoulders.

Firefly Scarf

The cables in this scarf are simple and beautiful, when staggered they resemble rivulets of water. The earthy tones of the yarn remind me of stones that have been splashed by water time and time again.

MATERIALS

Knitting loom

32-peg regular gauge knitting loom. Sample was knit using a yellow Knifty Knitter long loom.

Yarn

5 350 yards (320 m) bulky weight yarn. [Berroco Blackstone Tweed Chunky, 65% Wool, 25% Superkid Mohair, 10% Angora Rabbit Hair, in 2607 (A) and 2640 (B) colors, 130 yds (119 m) per 1.75 oz (50 g), was used in sample]

Tools

Tapestry needle
Cable needle
Knitting tool

Gauge

7 sts x 11 rows = 2 in (5 cm) in stitch pattern

4-st RC:
Sl 2 sts to cn and hold to back, k2, k2 from cn

Step 1 Skip peg 1 and peg 2 with yarn behind peg.
Step 2 Knit pegs 3 and 4.
Step 3 Remove stitches from pegs 3 and 4 and place on cable needle.
Step 4 Bring yarn to the front of peg 1 and knit peg 1. Knit peg 2.
Step 5 Move loop from peg 2 to peg 4.
Step 6 Move loop from peg 1 to peg 3.
Step 7 Place stitches from cable needle back on pegs 1 and 2. Gently pull on the working yarn to tighten cable.

Pattern notes
Use a single strand throughout.

Firefly Stitch Pattern
(shown in the green shaded area in chart below)
Row 1, 2, 4–10, 12–14, 16–22, 24: *p1, k4, p1, k4; rep from *
Row 3 & row 23: *p1, 4-st RC, p1, k4; rep from * (see side panel)
Row 11 & row 15: *p1, k4, p1, 4-st RC; rep from *

Directions
Edging
Using A, cast on 32 stitches and prepare to work a flat panel.
First row: Knit.
Next row: Purl.

Body
Continue working with A. Begin Firefly Stitch Pattern chart. Change yarn color at the beginning of chart row 21. Repeat Firefly chart rows 7 times. On the 7th repeat, do not change yarn at beginning of row 21. Keep working with A and continue to the following edging section.

Edging
Next row: Purl.
Next row: Knit.
Bind off with basic bind-off method. Weave ends in. Block lightly.

Entire scarf charted, including the garter stitch edging

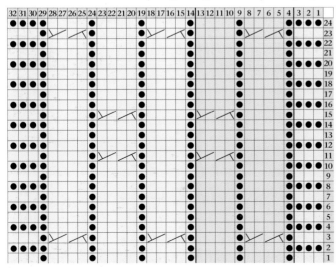

Knit
● Purl
⟋ 4-st RC

Carys Shrug

The perfect shrug to keep your shoulders warm without taking away from the dress. Loom knitted in a luscious beaded lace weight yarn this little number feels like it is barely there.

MATERIALS

Knitting loom

51-peg regular gauge knitting loom. Sample was knit using a blue Knifty Knitter long loom.

Yarn

🧶1 200 yards (183 m) lace weight yarn. [Symphony Lace, 63% kid mohair, 10% silk, 18% nylon, and 8% wool, in GoldenRod, 345 yds (315 m) per 2.8 oz (80 g), was used in sample]

Tools

Tapestry needle
Knitting tool
Stitch markers

Gauge

6 sts x 8 rows = 2 in (5 cm), blocked

Pattern notes

Worked as a flat panel. Use a single strand throughout.

Tip

For row 3: Place stitch markers, marking sets of 9 stitches, on the following pegs: 5 and 13, 14 and 22, 23 and 31, 32 and 40, 41 and 49.

For row 5: Place stitch markers, marking sets of 9 stitches, on the following pegs: 4 and 12, 13 and 21, 22 and 30, 31 and 39, 40 and 48.

Directions

Cast on 51 stitches and prepare to work as a flat panel.

Row 1: Knit.

Row 2: Knit.

Row 3: k4, *yo, k1, sl1—k1—psso, k2tog, k2, yo, k1; rep from * to the last 2 sts, k2.

Row 4: Knit.

Row 5: k3, *yo, k2, sl1—k1—psso, k2tog, k2, yo, k1; rep from * to the last 3 sts, k3.

Repeat rows 2–5 until item measures 26 inches (66 cm), or desired length, from cast-on edge. Bind off with basic bind-off method. Weave ends in. Steam block to 28 x 10 in (71 x 25 cm).

Assembly

Fold rectangle in half with RS facing in. With yarn threaded on a tapestry needle, create sleeves by sewing from each cuff, working toward the center for 3 inches (7.6 cm), leaving center 22 inches (56 cm) open. Weave in loose ends. Block lightly if needed.

BREAKDOWN

Row 3: k4, *yo, k2, sl1—k1—psso, k2tog, k2, yo, k1; rep from * to the last 2 sts, k2.

Row 5: k3, *yo, k2, sl1—k1—psso, k2tog, k2, yo, k1; rep from * to the last 3 sts, k3.

Over 9 stitches, if stitch markers were placed, each section is from stitch marker to stitch marker.

SECTION FROM *

Step 1 Lift loop from peg 4 and hold it. Move loop from peg 3 to peg 4. Place held loop back on peg 4 (two loops on peg 4).

Step 2 Move loop from peg 2 to peg 3.

Step 3 Move loop from peg 1 to peg 2.

Step 4: Lift loop from peg 5 and hold it. Move loop from peg 6 to peg 5. Place held loop back on peg 5 (two loops on peg 5).

Step 5: Move loop from peg 7 to peg 6.

Step 6: Move loop from peg 8 to peg 7.

Step 7: Peg 3 and peg 8 are empty.

Step 8: Knit peg 1 and peg 2.

Step 9: E-wrap peg 3.

Step 10: Knit peg 4 and peg 5 (treating both loops on pegs as one loop).

Step 11: Knit peg 6 and peg 7.

Step 12: E-wrap peg 8.

Step 13: Knit peg 9.

CrossOver Wrap

The CrossOver Wrap is an optical illusion wrap. It appears as it is one continuous wrap with a crossover at the front when in fact it is two flat panels joined at the back. Have fun loom knitting this wrap!

MATERIALS

Knitting loom

19- (23-, 27-) peg large gauge knitting loom. Sample was knit using a yellow Knifty Knitter round loom.

Yarn

(6) 360 yards (329 m) super bulky weight yarn. [Malabrigo Rasta, 100% merino, in Baya Electrica, 90 yds (82 m) per 5.3 oz (150 g), was used in sample]

Tools

Tapestry needle
Knitting tool

Gauge

5 sts x 8 rows = 2 inches (5 cm)

Size

S (M, L)

Pattern notes
Worked as a flat panel. Use a single strand throughout.

Special stitches
Sl1 wyif = Skip 1 peg with yarn in front of peg.
Sl1 wyib = Skip 1 peg with yarn in back of peg

Directions
Make 2
Cast on 19 (23, 27) stitches.
Row 1 k3, *sl1 wyif, k3; rep from * to the end.
Row 2 p1,*sl1 wyib, p3; rep from * to the last 2 sts, sl1 wyib, p1.
Work rows 1–2 until item measures 46 (48, 50) in/117 (122, 127) cm in length.

Bind off with basic removal method. Weave ends in. Block lightly.

Assembly
Step 1 Cross one scarf, then seam along one of the edges, leaving an opening at the center (where the scarf crosses) wide enough for the second scarf to pass through.
Step 2 Pass the second scarf through the opening created in step 1; seam along one of the edges. Join the ends of both scarf pieces at the back.

CHAPTER 5
Hats, Socks, and Mittens

Bluebells Hat

I love to work with color and this hat allows you to play with not just two colors but three. It is a fun design to loom knit, just be sure to work loosely.

MATERIALS

Knitting loom

60-peg regular gauge knitting loom. Sample was knit using a blue Knifty Knitter long loom and a Knifty Knitter loom clip.

Yarn

(5) 120 yards (110 m) bulky weight yarn. [Malabrigo Chunky, 100% merino, in Natural (A), Lettuce (B), and Busbando Azul (C), 104 yds (95 m) per 3.5 oz (100 g), was used in sample]

Tools

Tapestry needle
Knitting tool

Gauge

7 sts x 11 rows = 2 inches (5 cm)

Pattern note
Worked in the round. Use a single strand throughout.

Directions
Using A, cast on 60 stitches and join to work in the round.

Rnds 1–8: *k2, p2; rep from * .
Rnd 9–10: Knit.
Next: Work rows 1–19 from chart. Repeat pattern to complete each round.
Next 3 rnds: Using only A, knit.
Next rnd: *k2tog; rep from *

Bind off with gather bind-off method.
Weave in ends and block lightly.

Chart rows (read bottom to top):

19
18
17
16
15
14
13
12
11
10
9
8
7
6
5
4
3
2
1

Ribbed Beanie

This is the matching beanie to the ribbed scarf (page 52). The yarn is perfect for those who prefer a nice soft wool. Although the sample has only two colors, you could play around and add more stripes!

MATERIALS

Knitting loom

60-peg regular gauge knitting loom. Sample was knit using a blue Knifty Knitter long loom and a Knifty Knitter loom clip.

Yarn

(4) 110 yards (100 m) worsted weight yarn. [Berroco Pure Merino, 100% extra fine merino wool, in Black and Storm, 92 yds (85 m) per 1.75 oz (50 g), was used in sample]

Notions

Tapestry needle
Knitting tool

Gauge

8 sts x 12 rows = 2 in (5 cm) in rib stitch (stretched out).

Pattern note
Use a single strand throughout.

Rib Stitch Pattern
Row 1: *k2, p2; rep from *

Directions
Using the loom clip, set knitting loom to a 60-peg configuration. Using A, cast on 60 stitches and join to work in the round.

Work Rib Stitch Pattern until item measures 3 inches (7.6 cm) from the cast-on edge. Join B. Continue working in Rib Stitch Pattern until item measures 8 inches (20 cm) from the cast-on edge.
Next rnd: *k2tog; rep from *

Bind off with gather bind-off method.
Weave ends in and block lightly.

Iris Beanie

Hats do not need to be all stockinette or ribbed to make a warm accessory. The Iris Beanie uses a chunky weight wool that provides warmth and allows the lace design to shine.

MATERIALS

Knitting loom

48-peg large gauge knitting loom. Sample was knit using a purple round Knifty Knitter Loom.

Yarn

(5) 95 yards (87 m) bulky weight yarn. [Crystal Palace Chunky Mochi, 80% merino wool, 20% nylon, in Neptune, 49 yds (44 m) per 1.75 oz (50 g), was used in sample]

Tools

Tapestry needle
Knitting tool

Gauge

7 sts x 10 rows = 2 in (5 cm) in stitch pattern

Pattern note

Worked in the round. Use a single strand throughout.

Iris Stitch Pattern

Row 1: *k1, yo, sl1—k2tog—psso, yo, k4; rep from * (see side panel)
Rows 2, 4, 6: Knit.
Row 3: Repeat Row 1.
Row 5: *k5, yo, sl1—k2tog—psso, yo; rep from * (see side panel)

Directions

Brim

Cast on 48 stitches and join to work in the round.
Rnds 1–4: Knit.
Rnd 5: *k2tog, yo; rep from *
Rnds 6–9: Knit.
Rnd 10: Pick up the cast-on row and place the loops back on the pegs for a fold-over brim. Knit the row (treat both loops on each peg as one).

Body

Begin Iris Stitch Pattern. Repeat rows 1–6 of Iris Stitch Pattern until item measures 8 in (20 cm) from fold-over edge.
Next rnd: Knit.
Next rnd: *k2tog; rep from *.

Bind off with bind-off method. Weave ends in. Block lightly.

BREAK DOWN OF STITCH PATTERN ROWS

Row 1: *k1, yo, sl1—k2tog—psso, yo, k4; rep from *
Step 1 Knit peg 1.
Step 2 Move stitch from peg 3 to peg 4.
Step 3 Move stitch from peg 2 to peg 3.
Step 4 E-wrap peg 2.
Step 5 Skip peg 3 with yarn behind peg.
Step 6 Knit peg 4 (treat both loops on peg as one).
Step 7 Bring loop from peg 4 to peg 3.
Step 8 Lift bottom loop off peg 3.
Step 9 E-wrap peg 4.
Step 10 Knit pegs 5–8.

Row 5: *k5, yo, sl1—k2tog—psso, yo; rep from *
Step 1 Knit pegs 1–5.
Step 2 Move stitch from peg 7 to peg 8.
Step 3 Move stitch from peg 6 to peg 7.
Step 4 E–wrap peg 6.
Step 5 Skip peg 7 with yarn behind peg.
Step 6 Knit peg 8 (treat both loops on peg as one)
Step 7 Bring loop from peg 8 to peg 7.
Step 8 Lift bottom loop off peg 7.
Step 9 E-wrap peg 8.

Cloverleaf Slipper Socks

A toasty pair of slipper socks for her. A lovely lace pattern decorates the leg and simple stockinette forms the instep and sole for a comfortable pair of socks for relaxing in.

MATERIALS

Knitting loom

28-peg regular gauge knitting loom. Sample was knit using a yellow Knifty Knitter long loom and a Knifty Knitter loom clip.

Yarn

(5) 180 yards (164 m) bulky weight yarn. [Malabrigo Chunky, 100% merino, in Apple Green, 104 yds (95 m) per 3.5 oz (100 g), was used in sample]

Tools

Tapestry needle
Knitting tool
Two size 8 double-pointed needles (for grafting)

Gauge

7 sts x 11 rows = 2 in (5 cm)

Size

Female US shoe size 7, 8, 9

Clover Stitch Pattern

(worked over 7 stitches)
Rnds 1, 3, 5, 6: *p2, k3, p2; rep from *.
Rnd 2: *p2, yo, sl1—k2tog—psso, yo, p2; rep from * (see side panel).
Rnd 4: *p2, k1, yo, ssk, p2; rep from * (see side panel).

Directions

Using the loom clip, set knitting loom to a 28-peg configuration. Cast on 28 stitches and join to work in the round.

Cuff

Rnds 1–3: *p2, k3, p2; rep from *

Leg

Work rows 1–6 of Clover Stitch Pattern. Repeat 4 times, or until desired length for leg is reached. Work a short-row heel over 14 stitches (see side panel for short row instructions).
Knit 28 (32, 36) rounds.

Toe

Work a short-row toe over 14 stitches (see side panel)
Graft toes (see page 44).
Weave ends in. Block lightly.

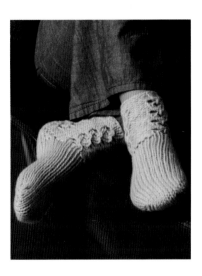

SHORT-ROW INSTRUCTIONS OVER 14 STITCHES

Knit to the 13th peg, W&T peg 14.
Knit to the 2nd peg, W&T peg 1.
Knit to the 12th peg, W&T peg 13.
Knit to the 3rd peg, W&T peg 2.
Knit to the 11th peg, W&T peg 12.
Knit to the 4th peg, W&T peg 3.
Knit to the 10th peg, W&T peg 11.
Knit to the 5th peg, W&T peg 4.
Knit to the 11th peg, (treating the loops on the peg as one loop). W&T peg 12.
Knit to the 4th peg, (treating loops as one). W&T peg 3.
Knit to the 12th peg, (treating loops as one). W&T peg 13.
Knit to the 3rd peg, (treating loops as one). W&T peg 2.
Knit to the 13th peg (treating loops as one). W&T peg 14.
Knit to the 2nd peg (treating loops as one). W&T peg 1.

BREAKDOWN OF STITCH PATTERN ROUNDS

Row 2: *p2, yo, sl1—k2tog—psso, yo, p2; rep from *

Step 1 Move loop from peg 4 to peg 5.

Step 2 Move loop from peg 3 to peg 4.

Step 3 Purl peg 1 and peg 2.

Step 4 E-wrap peg 3.

Step 5 Skip peg 4 with yarn toward back of peg.

Step 6 Knit peg 5 (treat both loops on peg as one loop).

Step 7 Move loop from peg 5 over to peg 4.

Step 8 Lift the bottom loop on peg 4 up and off of the peg.

Step 9 E-wrap peg 5.

Step 10 Purl pegs 6 and 7.

Row 4: *p2, k1, yo, ssk, p2; rep from *

Step 1 Purl peg 1 and peg 2.

Step 2 Knit peg 3.

Step 3 Lift loop from peg 5 and hold it.

Step 4 Lift loop from step and move it to peg 5.

Step 5 Place loop from peg 3 back on peg 5.

Step 6 E-wrap peg 4.

Step 7 Knit peg 5 (treat both loops on the peg as one loop).

Step 8 Purl pegs 6 and 7.

Twilled Slipper Socks

Toasty toes for him too! A simple twist in the stitches provides you with diagonals all around the cuff. The sole and instep are worked completely in stockinette to provide the wearer with cozy and warm socks.

Knitting loom

28-peg regular gauge knitting loom. Sample was knit using a yellow Knifty Knitter long loom and a Knifty Knitter loom clip.

Yarn

(5) 180 yards (164 m) bulky weight yarn. [Malabrigo Chunky, 100% merino, in Buscando Azul, 104 yds (95 m) per 3.5 oz (100 g), was used in sample]

Tools

Tapestry needle,
Knitting tool
Two size 8 double-pointed needles (for grafting)

Gauge

7 sts x 11 rows = 2 in (5 cm)

Size

Male US shoe size 7, 8, 9

Pattern notes

Use a single strand throughout.

Twilled Stripe Stitch Pattern:
Rnds 1, 3, 5, 7: *p1, k5, p1; rep from *
Rnd 4: *p1, k, LT, K2, P1; rep from *
Rnd 6: *p1, k2, LT, k1, p1.
Rnd 8: *p1, k3, LT, p1; rep from *

Directions

Using the loom clip, set knitting loom to a 28-peg configuration. Cast on 28 stitches and join to work in the round.

Cuff

Rnd 1–3: *p1, k5, p1; rep from *.

Leg

Work rounds 1–8 of Twilled Stripe Pattern. Repeat 4 times, or until desired length for leg is reached. Work a short-row heel over 14 stitches (see side panel on page 68 for short-row instructions).

BREAKDOWN OF LEFT TWIST (LT) – OVER 2 STITCHES
Step 1 Remove stitch from peg 2, hold at back of loom
Step 2 Remove loop from peg 1 and place on peg 2
Step 3 Place loop from step 1 on peg 1
Step 4 Skip peg 1
Step 5 Knit peg 2

Sole and instep

Continue working in the round in stockinette stitch (knit every round) until item measures 2 inches (5 cm) less than desired foot length.

Toe

Work a short-row toe over 14 stitches (see side panel on page 68 for short-row instructions). Graft toes (see page 44). Weave ends in. Block lightly.

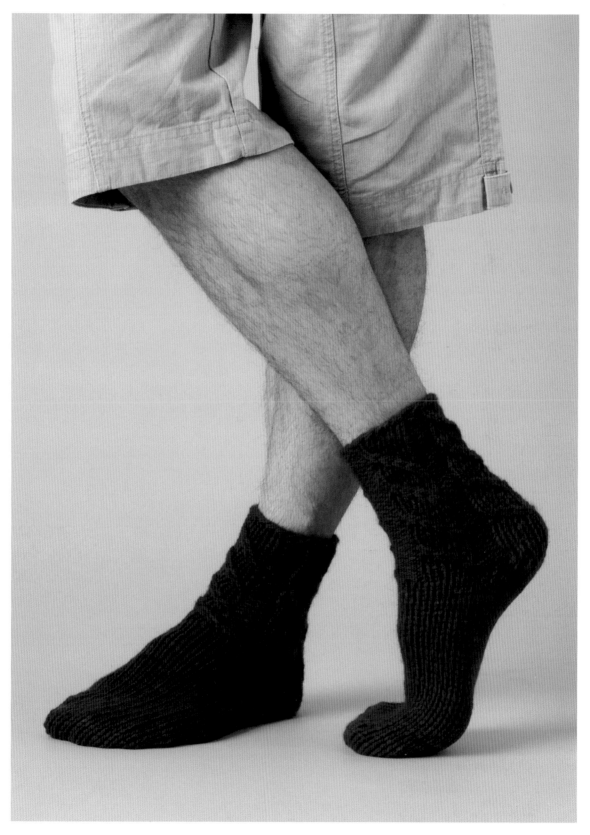

Family of Mittens

Toasty hands for the entire family. Delicate two-stitch cables wrap the wrist in warmth and simple stockinette make the body. Add a little bit of embroidery and different color yarns for an eye-catching contrast.

MATERIALS

Knitting loom

20-children (28-women, 32-men) peg regular gauge knitting loom. Sample was knit using a yellow Knifty Knitter Long Loom and a Knifty Knitter Loom Clip.

Yarn

(5) 90 (100, 130) yards, 82 (91, 118) m, bulky weight yarn.
Child sample: Malabrigo Chunky, 100% merino, in Sauterne (A), Fuchsia (B), and Apple Green (C), 104 yds (95 m) per 3.5 oz (100 g).
Adult sample: Berroco Blackstone Tweed Chunky, 65% Wool, 25% Superkid Mohair, 10% Angora Rabbit Hair, in Nor'Easter, 130 yds (119 m) per 1.75 oz (50 g).

Tools

Tapestry needle
Knitting tool
Stitch holder

Gauge

7.5 sts x 11 rows = 2 inches (5 cm) on 20-peg loom (7 sts x 11 rows = 2 inches (5 cm) on 28-, 32-peg loom)

Pattern notes

Worked in the round. Use a single strand throughout. Directions are given for child, adult women, and adult men sizes. The instructions for the adult mittens are inside parenthesis.

Special stitches

TW – Twist (See side panel).

Directions

Hand

Using the loom clip, set knitting loom to the desired peg configuration: 20 (28, 32).
Cast on 20 (28, 32) stitches and join to work in the round. For child size, use A to cast on.
Rnds 1–3: *k2, p2; rep from *
Rnd 4: *TW, p2; rep from *
Repeat rounds 1–4 three more times
For child size, join B.
Next 10 rounds: Knit.
Place the first 4 (5, 6) stitches on a stitch holder and drop them to the center of the loom. These stitches will be worked later, when creating the thumb.
Cast on 4 (5, 6) stitches on the emptied pegs.
Next 18 (30, 36) rnds: Knit.
Next rnd: *k2tog; rep from *
Bind off with gather bind-off method.

TW = TWIST WORKED OVER 2 STITCHES.

Step 1 Skip peg 1 with yarn behind peg.
Step 2 Knit peg 2. Hold newly formed loop with fingertips.
Step 3 Remove loop from peg 1 and move to peg 2.
Step 4 Place loop being held from Step 2 on peg 1.
Step 5 Skip peg 2 with yarn behind peg.

Thumb

Place the stitches from the stitch holder back on the loom.
Set the loom clip to the following peg configuration: 10 (12, 14) pegs. Pick up 1 stitch from the side of the thumb opening. Then pick up 4 (5, 6) stitches from the opposite side of the thumb opening. Pick up 1 additional stitch from the other side of the thumb opening. Now, 10 (12, 14) pegs have loops on them and the loom is prepared to create the thumb fabric.
Next 10 (16, 18) rnds: Knit.
Next rnd: *k2tog; rep from *
Bind off with gather removal method. Weave in ends and block lightly.

Optional embellishment

Add small Lazy Daisies to the body of the mitt, as shown on page 48: Single Chain Stitch.
Child size only: Connecting I-cord: work a 3-stitch I-cord: 45 in (114 cm.) Seam the I-cord to the cast-on edge on both mittens.

Lacy Wrist Warmers

The Lacy Wrist Warmers will keep your hands warm while freeing your fingers for typing or driving around.

MATERIALS

Knitting loom

24-peg regular gauge knitting loom. Sample was knit using a pink Knifty Knitter Long Loom and a Knifty Knitter Loom Clip.

Yarn

(5) 80 yards (73 m) bulky weight yarn. [Louet Gems Bulky, 100% merino wool, in Violet, 103 yds (93 m) per 3.5 oz (100 g), was used in sample]

Tools

Stitch holder
Stitch markers
Tapestry needle
Knitting tool

Gauge

7.5 sts x 11 rows = 2 in (5 cm)

Pattern notes

Worked in the round. Use single strand throughout.

Six Stitch Rib Stitch Pattern

Row 1: Knit.
Row 2: *yo, k1, sl1—k2tog—psso, k1, yo, k1; rep from * (see side panel).

Directions
Hand

Using the loom clip, set knitting loom to a 24-peg configuration. Cast on 24 stitches and join to work in the round.

Tip: Use stitch markers to mark 4 sets of 6 pegs each (Six Stitch Rib Stitch Pattern is worked over those sets of 6 stitches).

Work 6 repeats of the Six Stitch Rib Stitch Pattern.

Next 12 rnds: Knit.
Next rnd: Place the first 5 stitches on a stitch holder and drop them to the center of the loom. These stitches will be worked later, when creating the thumb. With the working yarn coming from the 19th peg, e-wrap the 5 empty pegs (there should be 24 wrapped pegs again).
Next 10 rnds: Knit.
Work 2 additional repeats of the Six Stitch Rib Stitch Pattern.
Bind off with basic removal method.

BREAKDOWN OF STITCH PATTERN ROW

Step 1 Move loop from peg 3 to 4.
Step 2 Move loop from peg 2 to 3.
Step 3 Move loop from peg 1 to 2.
Step 4 E-wrap peg 1.
Step 5 Knit peg 2.
Step 6 Skip peg 3 with yarn behind the peg.
Step 7 Knit peg 4, treating both loops on peg as one.
Step 8 Move loop from peg 4 to peg 3. Lift bottom loop over and off the peg.
Step 9 Knit peg 5 and move the loop to peg 4.
Step 10 E-wrap peg 5.
Step 11 Knit peg 6.

Thumb

Place the stitches from the stitch marker back on the loom. Set the loom clip to create a 12-peg configuration.
Pick up 1 stitch from the side of the thumb opening. Next, pick up 5 stitches from the opposite side of the thumb opening. Pick up 1 final stitch from the other side of the thumb opening. Now 12 pegs have loops on them and the loom is prepared to create the thumb fabric.
Next 4 rnds: Knit.
Bind off with basic bind-off method. Weave in ends and block lightly.

CHAPTER 6
Babies
and Toddlers

Children's Animal Hats: Bunny Hat

The Bunny Hat's soft and fuzzy ears knit with a plush yarn. Embroidered details make this bunny come alive.

MATERIALS

Knitting loom

60-peg regular gauge knitting loom. Sample was knit using a blue Knifty Knitter long loom and a Knifty Knitter loom clip.

Yarn

(5) 100 yards (91 m) bulky weight yarn. [Louet Gems Bulky, 100% merino wool, in Cream (80 yds) and Pink Panther (20 yds), 103 yds (93 m) per 3.5 oz (100 g); Berroco Plush, 100% nylon, in Crema, 90 yds (83 m) per 1.75 oz (50 g), was used in sample]

Tools

Tapestry needle
Knitting tool

Gauge

8 sts x 11 rows = 2 in (5 cm)

Pattern note

Hats are worked in the round. Accent pieces are worked as flat panels. Use a single strand throughout.

All three hats use the same basic hat design, simply worked in a different color for each animal. Choose the yarn color desired for the animal being created and follow the basic hat instructions, plus the additional sections for the animal chosen.

Directions

Basic Hat

Using the loom clip, set knitting loom to a 60-peg configuration. Using the desired color, cast on 60 stitches and join to work in the round.

Rnds 1–8: *k2, p2; rep from *.
Rnd 9: Knit.
Repeat round 9 until hat measures 7½ inches (19 cm) from cast-on edge.
Next rnd: *k2tog; rep from *.
Bind off with gather bind-off method. Weave in ends.
Block lightly.

Bunny Ears—Outer Layer

(make 2)
With the same yarn that was used to create the bunny hat, cast on 14 stitches.
Rows 1–9: Knit.
Row 10: K2tog, knit to last 2 sts, ssk.
Rows 11–17: Knit.
Row 18: Repeat row 10.
Rows 19–25: Knit.

Row 26: Repeat row 10.
Rows 27–29: Knit.
Row 30: Repeat row 10.
Row 31: Knit.
Row 32: Repeat row 10.
Row 33: k2tog, ssk.
Row 34: Knit.
Row 35: k2tog.
Bind off.

Bunny Ears—Inner Layer

(make 2)
Using the Berroco Plush yarn, cast on 10 stitches.
Rows 1–7: Knit.
Row 8: k2tog, knit to last 2 sts, ssk.
Rows 9–13: Knit.
Row 14: Repeat row 8.
Rows 15–19: Knit.
Row 20: Repeat row 8.
Rows 21–23: Knit.
Row 24: K2tog, SSK.
Row 25: Knit.
Row 26: K2tog.
Bind off.

Bunny Tail

Make a full, small pompom using the Berroco Plush yarn.

Assembly

Place an outer layer piece behind an inner layer piece, wrong sides facing each other. Backstitch the outer layer and inner layer together using the Pink Panther yarn. Repeat this step with the second set of ears.

Sew bunny ears to the top of the hat. Secure tail to the back of the hat. Weave in all yarn ends.

Little Duckling Hat

A little bill and webbed feet and cute little eyes decorate this duckling hat. This adorable hat will be a hit with children and adults alike.

MATERIALS

Knitting loom

60-peg regular gauge knitting loom. Sample was knit using a blue Knifty Knitter long loom and a Knifty Knitter loom clip.

Yarn

(5) 100 yards (91 m) bulky weight yarn. [Louet Gems Bulky, 100% merino wool, in Goldilocks (80 yds) and Terracotta (20 yds), 103 yds (93 m) per 3.5 oz (100 g), was used in sample]

Tools

Tapestry needle
Knitting tool
2 black buttons for eyes

Gauge

8 sts x 13 rows = 2 in (5 cm)

Size

Can stretch to an 18-inch (46-cm) circumference

Pattern note

One strand used throughout. Using the loom clip, set the knitting loom to a 60-peg configuration.

Directions

Using MC, cast on 60 sts, join to work in the round.
Rnds 1–6: *k2, p2; rep from * to the end.
Rnd 7: Knit.
Repeat round 7 until item measures 7 inches (18 cm) from cast-on edge. Bind off with gather bind-off method.
Weave ends in and block lightly.

Bill

Using CC, cast on 18 sts.
Row 1–5: k2, *p2, k2; rep from * to the end of row.
Row 6: k2tog, k to the last 2 sts, k2tog.
Bind off with basic bind-off method.

Legs

(make 2)
Using MC, cast on 2 sts.
Rows 1, 3, 5, 7, 9, 11: Knit.
Row 2: kfb, kfb.
Rows 4 & 6: kfb, k to last 2 sts; kfb.
Rows 8 & 10: ssk, k to last 2 sts, k2tog.
On remaining 4 sts, work 1½-inch (3.8-cm) I-cord.
Bind off with basic bind-off method.

Assembly

Sew the bill to the front of the hat. Sew the feet to the back of the hat. Make a slim pompom (about 6 to 8 strands of yarn) and attach to the top of the hat.
Sew buttons to the front of the hat. If making item for a very small child, you may prefer to embroider the eyes.

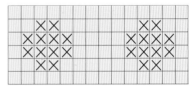

Little Lamb Hat

Soft and plush yarn makes this hat the softest ever! A cute little bow decorates the hat.

MATERIALS

Knitting loom

60-peg regular gauge knitting loom. Sample was knit using a blue Knifty Knitter long loom and a Knifty Knitter loom clip.

Yarn

(5) (4) 80 yards (73 m) bulky weight yarn and 30 yards (27 m) worsted weight yarn. [Berroco Plush, 100% nylon, in Crema, 90 yds (83 m) per 1.75 oz (50 g); Malabrigo worsted, 100% merino wool, in Simple Taupe, 215 yds (196 m) per 3.5 oz (100 g), was used in sample]

Tools

Cable Needle
Tapestry needle
Knitting tool

Size

Can stretch to an 18-in (46-cm) circumference

Pattern notes

One strand used throughout. Using the loom clip, set the knitting loom to a 60-peg configuration.

Directions

Using A, cast on 60 sts, join to work in the round.
Rnds 1–6: *k2, p2; rep from * to the end.
Rnd 7: Knit.
Repeat round 7 until item measures 7 inches (18 cm) from cast-on edge. Bind off with gather bind-off method.
Weave ends in and block lightly.

Fluffy Ears

(make 2)
Using A, cast on 10.
Row 1–4: Knit.
Row 5: k2tog, k to last 2 sts, k2tog.
Row 6: Knit.
Row 7: Rep row 5.
Row 8: Knit.
Row 9: Rep row 5.
Row 10: Knit.
Bind off with basic removal method.

Inner Ears

(make 2)
Using B, cast on 12.
Row 1–4: Knit.
Row 5: k2tog, k to last 2 sts, k2tog.
Row 6: Knit.
Row 7: Rep row 5.
Row 8: Knit.
Row 9: Rep row 5.
Row 10: Knit.
Row 11: Rep row 5.
Row 12: Knit.
Bind off with basic bind-off method.

Assembly

Place ear panels wrong side facing and sew them together. Using A, attach ears to sides of hat.

Bow

Using B, cast on 9.
Row 1: *k1, p1; rep from * to last st, k1.
Row 2: *p1, k1; rep from * to last st, p1.
Repeat rows 1–2 fifteen more times. Bind off with basic bind-off method.

Assembly

Thread tapestry needle with B, cinch the center of the bow panel and secure with a couple of stitches. Place the bow below one of the ears on the hat. Secure to the hat with a couple of stitches.

Baby's First Mitts and Socks

A set of little mitts and socks to keep your baby warm. They are both knit in simple stockinette to keep the pattern simple and fast.

MATERIALS

Knitting loom

24-peg regular gauge knitting loom. Sample was knit using a yellow Knifty Knitter long loom and a Knifty Knitter loom clip.

Yarn

(5) 120 yards (110 m) bulky weight yarn. [Debbie Bliss Cashmerino Chunky, 55% merino wool, 10% cashmere, 35% microfiber, in Fuchsia, 72 yds (65 m) per 1.75 oz (50 g), was used in sample]

Notions

Tapestry needle
Knitting tool

Gauge

9 sts x 12 rows = 2 in (5 cm)

Size

0–3 months (3–6, 6–9)

Pattern notes

Worked in the round. Use a single strand throughout.

Directions

MITTS

(make 2)
Using the loom clip, set knitting loom to a 20- (20-, 24-) peg configuration.
Cast on 20 (20, 24) stitches and join to work in the round.
Rnds 1–6: *k2, p2; rep from *.
Rnds 7–21 (7–23, 7–24): Knit.
Next rnd: *k2tog; rep from *.
Bind off with gather bind-off method.

SOCKS

(make 2)
Cast on 20 (24, 24) stitches and join to work in the round.

Cuff
Rnds 1–6: *k2, p2; rep from *

Leg
Rnd 7–14: Knit.
Work a short-row heel over 10 (12, 12) stitches (see side panel).

Sole and Instep
Next 12 (14, 16) rnds: Knit.
Work a short-row toe over 10 (12, 12) stitches (see side panel).

Graft toes (see page 44)
Weave ends in. Block lightly.

SHORT-ROW INSTRUCTIONS OVER 12 STITCHES

Knit to the 11th peg, W&T peg 12.
Knit to the 2nd peg, W&T peg 1.
Knit to the 10th peg, W&T peg 11.
Knit to the 3rd peg, W&T peg 2.
Knit to the 9th peg, W&T peg 10.
Knit to the 4th peg, W&T peg 3.
Knit to the 10th peg (treating the loops on the peg as one loop), W&T peg 11.
Knit to the 3rd peg (treating the loops on the peg as one loop), W&T peg 2.
Knit to the 11th peg (treating the loops on the peg as one loop), W&T peg 12.
Knit to the 2nd peg (treating the loops on the peg as one loop), W&T peg 1.

Heel: Continue working the instep and sole as instructed in pattern—be sure to pick up the extra loops on each of the pegs on the next round.

Toe: Continue on to the grafting portion of the pattern.

SHORT-ROW INSTRUCTIONS OVER 10 STITCHES

Knit to the 9th peg, W&T peg 10.
Knit to the 2nd peg, W&T peg 1.
Knit to the 8th peg, W&T peg 9.
Knit to the 3rd peg, W&T peg 2.
Knit to the 7th peg, W&T peg 8.
Knit to the 4th peg, W&T peg 3.
Knit to the 8th peg (treating the loops on the peg as one loop), W&T peg 9.
Knit to the 3rd peg (treating the loops on the peg as one loop), W&T peg 2.
Knit to the 9th peg (treating the loops on the peg as one loop), W&T peg 10.
Knit to the 2nd peg (treating the loops on the peg as one loop), W&T peg 1.

Heel: Continue working the instep and sole as instructed in pattern—be sure to pick up the extra loops on each of the pegs on the next round.

Toe: Continue on to the grafting portion of the pattern.

Braid Circular Blanket

Short row shaping makes this circular blanket possible. The blanket is knit in short-row wedges that are worked continuously, then when fifteen wedges have been completed, the cast on edge is seamed to the bind-off edge. Finish with a decorative cable braid.

MATERIALS

Knitting loom

61-peg regular gauge knitting loom. Sample was knit using a blue Knifty Knitter long loom.

Yarn

(5) 800 yards (730 m) bulky weight yarn. [Berroco Comfort Chunky, 50% superfine nylon, 50% superfine acrylic, in Barley (A), 3 skeins, Grape Jelly (B), 2 skeins, and Aegean Sea (C), 2 skeins, 150 yds (138 m) per 3.5 oz (100 g), was used in sample]

Notions

Knitting tool
Cable needle (for braid)
Tapestry needle
19 stitch markers

Gauge

7 sts x 12 rows = 2 in (5 cm)

Size

20-in (51-cm) radius

Pattern notes

One strand throughout. Worked as a flat panel with short rows. Braid knitted separately and then sewn to the blanket.

Special stitches

W&T = Lift the loop on the peg with stitch marker, e-wrap the peg, place loop back on peg.

Directions

Place stitch markers on the following pegs: 3, 6, 9, 12, 15, 18, 21, 24, 27, 30, 33, 36, 39, 42, 45, 48, 51, 54, and 57).
Using A, cast on 61 sts.
Row 1: Purl to the end of the row.
***Row 2:** Knit to last 4 sts, W on the peg with the stitch marker. W&T.
Row 3: Purl to the end of row.
Row 4: Knit to within 3 sts of the peg with the stitch marker. W on the peg with the stitch marker. W&T. Repeat rows 3–4 until only 4 stitches remain.
Next row: p4.*

There should be a pair of stitches between stitch markers all along the loom. The knitted fabric should resemble a pie-shaped panel. Change to B, begin next wedge: Purl to the end of the row (The blanket is knit in short-row wedges that are worked continuously, then when fifteen wedges have been completed, the cast on edge is seamed to the bound off edge).

Repeat from * to *.
Change to C, begin next wedge. Repeat from * to *.
Repeat last 3 wedges 4 more times for a total of 15 wedges. Bind off with basic bind-off method. Using mattress stitch, sew the cast-on edge to the bind-off edge. Run yarn through the hole at the center and cinch close. Weave ends in and block.

Braid

Using A, cast on 8 sts.
Row 1: k3, c4b, k1.
Row 2: p1, k6, p1.
Row 3: k1, c4f, k3.
Row 4: p1, k6, p1.

Repeat rows 1–4 until braid measures 120 in (305 cm), or blanket circumference. Bind off with basic bind-off method.

Finishing

Using mattress stitch, sew braid to outer edge of the blanket.

Stroller Baby Blanket

Your baby will love the softness of this pima cotton blanket!
Knit in 5 strips, then seamed together. A simple crochet
edging adds decoration.

MATERIALS

Knitting loom

25-peg fine gauge knitting loom.
Sample was knit using a Décor
Accents adult sock fine gauge
loom. Any other loom with a
peg set of ¼ an inch (1 cm)
can be used

Yarn

2 690 yards (630 m) sports
weight yarn. [Berroco Pure Pima
Cotton, in Barely Blue (A),
1 skein, Limelight (B), 1 skein,
Oyster (C), 1 skein, Mazzarine
(D), 1 skein, Beech (E), 1 skein,
and White Linen (F), 1 skein,
115 yds (105 m) per 1.75 oz
(50 g), was used in sample]

Tools

Knitting tool
G-6 (4 mm) crochet hook for
crochet edging
Tapestry needle

Gauge

10 sts x 14 rows = 2 in (5cm)

Size

26 x 24 in (66 x 60 cm)

Pattern notes

One strand throughout. Worked in
5 separate panels.

Directions

Hand

Panel 1

Cast on 25 sts.
Using A, knit 30 rows. Cut yarn. Join B.
Using B, knit 30 rows. Cut yarn. Join C.
Using C, knit 30 rows. Cut yarn. Join D.
Using D, knit 30 rows. Cut yarn. Join E.
Using E, knit 30 rows. Cut yarn. Join F.
Using F, knit 30 rows. Cut yarn.
Bind off with basic bind-off method.
Steam block and set aside.

Panel 2

Cast on 25 sts.
Using B, knit 30 rows. Cut yarn. Join C.
Using C, knit 30 rows. Cut yarn. Join D.
Using D, knit 30 rows. Cut yarn. Join E.
Using E, knit 30 rows. Cut yarn. Join F.
Using F, knit 30 rows. Cut yarn. Join A.
Using A, knit 30 rows. Cut yarn.
Bind off with basic bind-off method.
Steam block and set aside.

Panel 3

Cast on 25 sts.
Using C, knit 30 rows. Cut yarn. Join D.
Using D, knit 30 rows. Cut yarn. Join E.
Using E, knit 30 rows. Cut yarn. Join F.
Using F, knit 30 rows. Cut yarn. Join A.
Using A, knit 30 rows. Cut yarn. Join B.
Using B, knit 30 rows. Cut yarn.
Bind off with basic bind-off method.
Steam block and set aside.

Panel 4

Cast on 25 sts.
Using D, knit 30 rows. Cut yarn. Join E.
Using E, knit 30 rows. Cut yarn. Join F.
Using F, knit 30 rows. Cut yarn. Join A.
Using A, knit 30 rows. Cut yarn. Join B.
Using B, knit 30 rows. Cut yarn. Join C.
Using C, knit 30 rows. Cut yarn.
Bind off with basic bind-off method.
Steam block and set aside.

Panel 5

Cast on 25 sts.
Using E, knit 30 rows. Cut yarn. Join F.
Using F, knit 30 rows. Cut yarn. Join A.
Using A, knit 30 rows. Cut yarn. Join B.
Using B, knit 30 rows. Cut yarn. Join C.
Using C, knit 30 rows. Cut yarn. Join D.
Using D, knit 30 rows. Cut yarn.
Bind off with basic bind-off method.
Steam block and set aside.

Finishing

Using mattress stitch, sew panel 1 to
panel 2, sew panel 3 to panel 2, sew
panel 4 to panel 3, sew panel 5 to
panel 4 (use diagram if needed).
Weave ends in and block lightly.

Edging

Using crochet hook single crochet
around the perimeter of the blanket.

F	E	D	C	B
E	D	C	B	A
D	C	B	A	F
C	B	A	F	E
B	A	F	E	D
A	F	E	D	C

Mr. & Mrs. Frosty

Get in the festive spirit of wintertime with Mr. & Mrs. Frosty. Now even if you do not get snow, you can have your very own snowmen.

MATERIALS

Knitting loom

24-peg regular gauge knitting loom. Sample was knit using a yellow Knifty Knitter long loom and a Knifty Knitter loom clip.

Yarn

(5) 80 yards (73 m) bulky weight yarn. [Berroco Plush, 100% nylon, in Crema (body), 90 yds (83 m) per 1.75 oz (50 g); Berroco Pure Merino Wool, 100% extra fine merino wool, in Storm and Bluebell (hat), in Ballerina (Scarf and Earmuffs), in Black Magic (accents), and in Paprika (nose), 92 yds (85 m) per 1.75 oz (50 g); was used in sample]

Tools

Tapestry needle
Knitting tool
Crochet hook

Pattern note

Use a single strand throughout.

Directions

Body

Using the loom clip, set knitting loom to a 24-peg configuration. Using Berroco Plush, cast on 24 stitches and join to work in the round.

Round 1: Knit.

Repeat round 1 until item measures 4 inches (10 cm) from cast-on edge.

Next round: *k2tog; rep from * to the end of round.

Next round: *yo, k1; rep from * to the end of round.

Repeat round 1 until item measures 7½ inches (19 cm) from cast-on edge.

Next round: *k2tog; rep from * to the end of round.

Bind off with gather bind-off method.

Embroidery

Eyes: Using E, make a French knot for each eye on the upper portion of the body.

Nose: Using F, crochet eight chains. Join the beginning stitch to the last stitch closing the circle. Stitch the circle closed. Secure the nose to the face. Be sure to center it, using the eyes as a guide.

Buttons: Using B (D for Earmuff Frosty), double stitch three times in the lower portion of the body. Use the eyes as guides to center the buttons vertically down the body.

Hat

Using the loom clip, set knitting loom to a 32-peg configuration. Using B, cast on 32 stitches and join to work in the round.

Rounds 1–4: *k2, p2; rep from * to the end.

Rounds 5 & 6: Join C, knit.

Rounds 7 & 8: Join B, knit. Repeat last 4 rounds two more times.

Next round: *k2tog; rep from * Bind off with gather removal method. Using both B and C, make a small pompom. Secure to the top of the hat.

Scarves
Striped scarf

Cast on 6 stitches and prepare to work a flat panel.

Row 1: Using color B, p1, k4, p1.

Row 2: Knit.

Row 3: Using color C, p1, k4, p1.

Row 4: Knit.

Repeat last 4 rows until item measures 12 inches (30 cm) from cast-on edge.

Bind off with basic bind-off method. Weave ends in.

Create 10 sets of simple fringes using both colors. Attach fringes to both ends of the scarf.

Solid scarf

Cast on 6 stitches and prepare to work a flat panel.

Row 1: Using color D, p1, k4, p1.

Row 2: Knit.

Repeat rows 1–2 until item measures 12 inches (30 cm) from cast-on edge.

Bind off with basic bind-off method. Weave ends in.

Create 10 sets of simple fringes. Attach fringes to both ends of the scarf.

Earmuffs

Using D cast on 12 stitches and prepare to work a flat panel.

Row 1–6: Knit.

Remove with gather bind-off method, leaving a long tail. Using the long tail, seam the side using mattress stitch, then sew the cast-on edge closed. Shape into a small pinwheel. Make a second pinwheel following the same instructions. Using D, create a 3-stitch I-cord measuring 4 inches (10 cm) long. Secure a pinwheel at each end of the I-cord.

Assembly

Fill each Frosty body with polyester filling, shaping them as you stuff them. Using the tapestry needle, gather the opening and sew it closed. To dress each Frosty, secure the scarf at the midpoint of the body and head and secure the hat, or the earmuffs, to the top of the head.

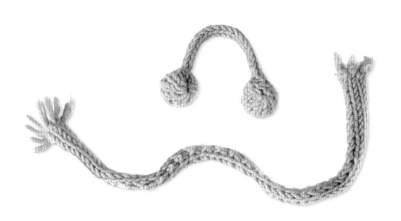

CHAPTER 7
Totes, Bags, Holders, and Boxes

Flowers Felted Bag

A little whimsical bag with flowers and needle felting to bring a simple bag to life!

MATERIALS

Knitting loom

36-peg regular gauge knitting loom. Sample was knit using a blue Knifty Knitter long loom.

Yarn

(5) 200 yards (182 m) bulky weight yarn. [Lamb's Pride Bulky, 85% wool, 15% mohair, in Caribbean Waves, 100 yards (bag), in Ruby Red, 30 yards (red flowers), in Cream, 20 yards (cream flower), 125 yds (114 m) per 4 oz (113 g), was used in sample].

Tools

Tapestry needle
Knitting tool

Gauge

6 sts x 10 rows = 2 in (5 cm), pre-felted

Size

11 x 11 in (28 x 28 cm), pre-felted; 9 x 8 in (23 x 20 cm), felted

Directions

BAG (make 2)
Cast on 36 stitches.
Row 1–8: Knit.
Row 9: k2tog, k to the last 2 sts, k2tog.
Repeat rows 1–9 four more times (26 sts remain).
Next row: Knit.
Next row: Purl.
Place panels with the wrong sides together. Sew both panels together using mattress stitch.

HANDLE

Cast on 4 stitches. Work an I-cord over the 4 stitches to create a 12-inch long cord. Sew the handle to the side corners of the bag.

BIG RED FLOWER

Cast on 5 stitches.
Small petal
Row 1: kfb, k4.
Row 2: k4, kfb, k1.
Row 3 & 4: k7.
Row 5: k1, k2tog, k4.
Row 6: k3, k2tog, k1.
Repeat rows 1–6 three times more.
Do not break yarn.
Medium petal
Rows 1 & 3: kfb, k to end.
Rows 2 & 4: k to last 2 sts, kfb, k1.
Rows 5–8: Knit.
Rows 9 & 11: k1, k2tog, k to end.
Rows 10 & 12: k to last 3 sts, k2tog, k1.
Repeat rows 1–12 two times more.
Break yarn.

SMALL RED FLOWER

Follow instructions for big red flower, stopping after one repetition of the medium petal.

SMALL WHITE FLOWER

Follow instructions for big red flower, completing only the small petal portion.
Weave ends in.

Assembly

Thread a tapestry needle with the same color yarn as the flower. Make a running stitch along the straight edge of the panel. Pull on the yarn tails to gather and form the knitted fabric into a flower shape. Tie the yarn tails together to secure. Weave ends in.

Felting

For Felting instuctions, see page 105.

Needle Felting (shown at right)

Once your bag is completely dry, use a needle felting kit, including a special barbed needle and foam, to decorate your bag. Felt the swirls onto the bag as in the finished picture, right.

Finishing

When the bag and flowers have completely dried, secure the flowers to the right side of the bag, in the upper corner. Attach handles to the bag by sewing them on.

Starry Night Bag

The Starry Night Bag, is an evening bag with bead accents. A purse frame makes this bag one of a kind. The threading of the beads is a little time consuming, but so worth it!

MATERIALS

Knitting loom

43-peg regular gauge knitting loom. Sample was knit using a blue Knifty Knitter long loom.

Yarn

4 150 yards (137 m) worsted weight yarn. [Louet MerLin, 70% merino wool, 30% wet spun linen, in Steel Gray, 156 yds (142 m) per 3.5 oz (100 g), was used in sample]

Tools

Tapestry needle
Knitting tool
Beading needle
182 seed beads (size 6R)
Purse frame rods

Gauge

10.5sts x 12 rows = 2 in (5 cm)

Size

9 x 8 in (23 x 20 cm)

Stitch pattern
Quilted Beaded Stockinette Pattern:

Q1 (quilt 1): Pick up the loose strand of yarn that is resting in front of the pegs and place on the peg that is to be worked. Knit the peg, treating the strand and the loop on the peg as one loop.

Rows 1, 3, 5, 7: Knit.

Row 2: k4, * skip 5 stitches with yarn in front of pegs—slide bead, k1; rep from * to the last 3 stitches, k3.

Row 4: k6, *Q1, k5; rep from * to the last 7sts, Q1, k6.

Row 6: k3, skip 3 stitches with yarn in front of pegs—slide bead, *k1, skip 5 stitches with yarn in front of pegs—slide bead; rep from * to the last 7 sts, k1, skip 3 stitches with yarn in front of pegs—slide bead, k3.

Row 8: k3, *Q1, k5; rep from * to the last 4sts, Q1, k3.

Directions

Using a beading needle, thread the beads onto the yarn.

Bag

Cast on 43 stitches and prepare to work a flat panel.

Seed Stitch Border:

Row 1: *k1, p1; rep from * to last st, k1.

Row 2: *p1, k1; rep from * to last st, p1.

Repeat rows 1–2 seven times more (16 rows total).

Next 56 rows: Work in Quilted Beaded Stockinette.

Next 4 rows: Work row 1 and row 2 of the Seed Stitch Border two times.

Next 56 rows: Work in Quilted Beaded Stockinette.

Next 16 rows: Repeat Seed Stitch Border.

Bind off with basic bind-off method. Weave in ends and steam block. After the item is blocked, pop the beads to the right side of the work, using the knitting tool to gently push them to the right side of the fabric.

Lining (optional)

Sew a rectangle panel of fabric 9 x 8½ in (23 x 22 cm). Secure the lining to the inside of the bag.

Finishing

Step 1: To form the pocket for the frame rods to pass through, place the knitted fabric right side down. Fold the seed stitch section in half, forming the pocket. Secure in place by sewing the cast-on edge down to the wrong side of the fabric. Repeat with the other end of fabric.

Step 2: To form the bag, place the knitted fabric right side down. Fold the fabric in half. Using the tapestry needle, mattress stitch close the quilted section of the bag.

Step 3: Pass the frame rods through the pockets formed in step 1. Secure the rods onto the bag.

Lexi Bag

The Lexi bag is knit in three panels that are seamed together. A ribbon passed through the eyelets make the little bag pop!

MATERIALS

Knitting loom

Large Gauge Knitting Loom. Knifty Knitter Green Round Loom or any other loom with at least 21 pegs.

Yarn

(5) 250 yards (228 m) bulky weight yarn. [Debbie Bliss Cashmerino Chunky, 55% merino wool, 10% cashmere, 35% microfiber, in Fuschia, 72 yds (65 m) per 1.75 oz (50 g), was used in sample]

Tools

Tapestry needle
Knitting tool
2 yards of ½ inch wide Gross Grain Black Ribbon.
D Shape handles (7 in width x 4.5 in height)

Gauge

6 sts x 10 rows = 2 in stockinette stitch

Size

7 in x 7½ in x 3½ in (not including handles)

Pattern notes

Use 2 strands of yarn as one throughout the pattern.
Always skip (slip) the first stitch of every row.

Directions

Front & Back Panels

(make 2)
Cast on 21 stitches (recommend e-wrap cast on).
Rows 1–21: Sl1, k to the end of the row
Row 22: Sl1, *yo, k2tog; rep from * to the end of row
Row 23: Sl1, *k1, p1; rep from * to last 2sts, k2
Row 24: Sl1, *p1, k1; rep from * to the end of the row
Rows 25-42: Rep Rows 23 and 24.
Bind Off with basic bind off method.

Side panel

Cast on 10 stitches
Rows 1–74: Sl1, k to the end.
Bind off with basic bind off method.

Assembly

Panels Seam the side panel to the front and back panels with mattress stitch.
Handles Position one of the handles on the wrong side of the back panel (close to the top). Pass the knitted fabric through the opening of the handle; fold the fabric over the handle so that it covers the bottom portion of the handle. Seam the handle in place. Repeat with the other handle.

Ribbon

Pass the ribbon through the eyelets of the bag and position it as desired. Make a bow with the two ends of the ribbon. Trim and position the bow as desired on the bag.

Knick-knack Boxes

We all have little knick-knacks all over the house, create little felted boxes to house all the little odds and ends.

MATERIALS

Knitting loom

22-peg large gauge knitting loom. Sample was knit using a yellow Knifty Knitter round loom.

Yarn

(5) 45 yards (41 m) bulky weight yarn. [Lamb's Pride Bulky, 85% wool, 15% mohair, in Fuchsia (pink sample), and in Limeade (green sample), 125 yds (114 m) per 4 oz (113 g), was used in samples]

Tools

Tapestry needle
Knitting tool

Gauge

7 sts x 8 rows = 2 in (5 cm)

Size

Jewelry box: 5 x 6 inches (12½ x 15 cm), pre-felted;| 4½ x 5 in (11 x 12.5 cm), felted
Business card holder: 3 x 5 in (7.6 x 12½ cm), pre-felted; 21/2 x 4.5 in (6 x 11 cm), felted

Pattern notes

One strand throughout. Worked as a flat panel. Use the e-wrap to cast on the desired number of stitches.

Garter Stitch (GS) Pattern:

Row 1: Knit.
Row 2: Purl.
Rows 1 & 2 make one Garter Stitch Ridge.

Directions

JEWELRY BOX

CO 12 sts
Row 1–10: Work 5 GS ridges.
Row 11: CO 5 at beginning of row. Knit to the end (17 sts on loom).
Row 12: CO 5 at beginning of row. Purl to the end (22sts on loom).
Row 13–26: Work 7 GS ridges.
Row 27: BO 5 at beginning of row. Knit to the end (17sts remain on loom).
Row 28: BO 5 at beginning of row. Purl to the end (12sts remain on loom).
Row 29–38: Work 5 GS ridges. Bind off with basic bind-off method.

Finishing

Seam each of the short sides to each other (see diagram). Even unfelted, the box is strong enough to hold odds & ends! Felt and block dry. (See side panel right)

BUSINESS CARD HOLDER

CO 12sts.

Row 1, 3, 5, 7, 9: Knit.

Row 2, 4, 6, 8, 10: Purl.

Row 11: CO 5 at beginning of row. Knit to the end (17 sts on loom).

Row 12: CO 5 at beginning of row. Purl to the end (22 sts on loom).

Row 13, 15, 17, 19: Knit.

Row 14, 16, 18, 20: Purl.

Row 21: BO 5 at beginning of row. Knit to the end (17 sts remain on loom).

Row 22: BO 5 at beginning of row. Purl to the end (12 sts remain on loom).

Row 23, 25, 27, 29, 31: Knit.

Row 24, 26, 28, 30, 32: Purl.

Bind off with basic bind-off method.

FELTING

Step 1 Set top-load washer to hot water, small load.

Step 2 Add 1 tablespoon of wool detergent or baby shampoo.

Step 3 Place item inside a zippered pillowcase. Place the pillowcase in the washer along with two pairs of jeans to aid in agitation.

Step 4 Let the cycle run for about 10 minutes and check progress. If box is not desired size, place inside the pillowcase again and wash for a few more minutes.

Step 5 When the item reaches desired effect/size, take out and shape (you may put something inside to help in obtaining desired shape). Allow to air dry for about 24–48 hours.

Pencil Holder

Make a matching pencil holder to go with the business card holder. Embellishments made with needle felting make this home accessory pop!

MATERIALS

Knitting loom

31-peg large gauge knitting loom. Sample was knitted using a red Knifty Knitter round loom.

Yarn

(5) 55 yards (50 m) bulky weight yarn. [Lamb's Pride Bulky, 85% wool, 15% mohair, in Caribbean Waves (MC), Limeade (CC) 1 yard, and Fuchsia (SCC) 1 yard, 125 yds (114 m) per 4 oz (113 g), was used in sample]

Tools

Tapestry needle
Knitting tool

Gauge

7 sts x 8 rows = 2 in (5cm)

Size

10 x 8 in (25 x 20 cm), pre-felted; 9 x 7 in (23 x 18 cm), felted

Pattern notes

One strand throughout. Worked in the round.

Directions

Using MC, cast on 31 sts, join to work in the round.
Round 1: Knit.
Rep round 1 until item measures 8 inches (20 cm) from cast-on edge
Next round: *k2tog; rep from * to the end of round.
Bind off with gather bind-off method.

If you wish to decorate the pencil holder, needle felt the wave with CC. Using SCC, needle felt the dots at the dips of the waves.

FELTING

Step 1 Set top-load washer (top loader) to hot water, small load.
Step 2 Add 1 tablespoon of wool detergent or baby shampoo.
Step 3 Place item inside a zippered pillowcase. Place the pillowcase in the washer along with two pairs of jeans to aid in agitation.
Step 4 Let the cycle run for about 10 minutes and check progress. If item is not desired size, place inside the pillowcase again and wash for a few more minutes.
Step 5 When the item reaches desired effect/size, take out and shape (you may put something inside to help in obtaining desired shape). Allow to air dry for about 24–48 hours.

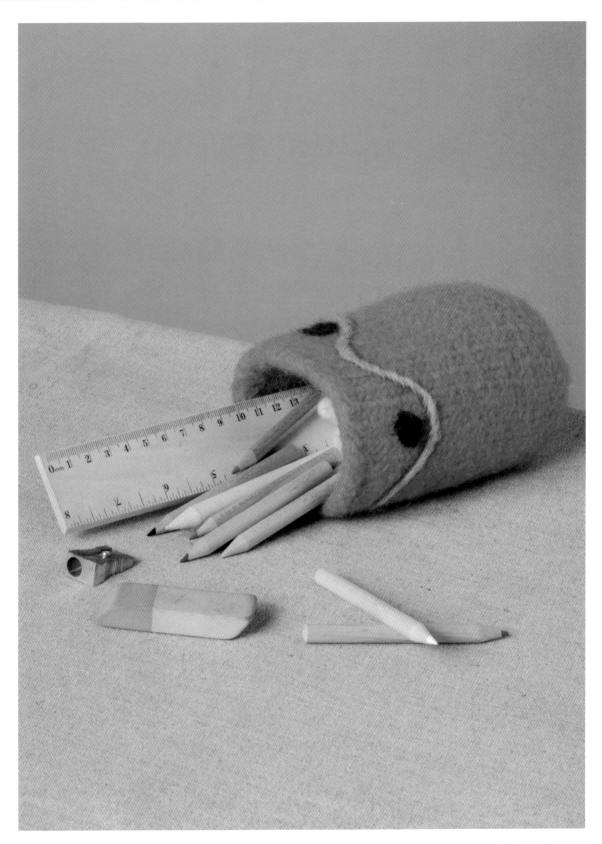

Cell Phone Cozy

Protect your cell phone with a decorative cell phone cozy. Loom knitted then felted to provide extra protection to your cell phone.

MATERIALS

Knitting loom

14 peg large gauge knitting loom. Sample was knit using a red Knifty Knitter round loom.

Yarn

(5) 55 yards (50 m) bulky weight yarn. [Lamb's Pride Bulky, 85% wool, 15% mohair, in Caribbean Waves (MC) 40 yards, Limeade (CC) 15 yards, 125 yds (114 m) per 4 oz (113 g), was used in sample]

Tools

Tapestry needle
Knitting tool
1 decorative button

Gauge

7 sts and 8 rows to 2 in (5cm)

Size

Pre-felted: 5 x 4 in
Felted: 4½ x 3 in

Pattern Notes

One strand throughout.
Worked as a flat panel.

Directions

Using MC, cast on 14 sts.
Using MC: **Rows 1–8**: k
Join CC. **Rows 9-10**: k
*Pick up MC. **Rows 11–14**: k
Pick up CC: **Rows 15–16**: k*
Rep from * to * : 2 more times
Next 8 rows, pick up MC: k
Bind off with basic bind-off method
Fold panel in half. Sew sides closed using mattress stitch.

Handle

Using MC, work a 3-stitch I-cord:
6 in (15 cm)
Attach I-cord at the side seams of the bag.

Button loop

Using MC, crochet a 4-in chain.
Attach the button loop at the middle of the cozy opening.

FELTING

Step 1 Set top-load washer to hot water, small load.

Step 2 Add 1 tablespoon of wool detergent or baby shampoo.

Step 3 Place item inside a zippered pillowcase. Place the pillowcase in the washer along with two pairs of jeans to aid in agitation.

Step 4 Let the cycle run for about 10 minutes and check progress. If item is not desired size, place inside the pillowcase again and wash for a few more minutes.

Step 5 When the item reaches desired effect/size, take out and shape (you may put something inside to help in obtaining desired shape). Allow to air dry for about 24–48 hours.

CHAPTER 8
Around the House

Aran Lapghan

A simple crossing of stitches make the design of this lapghan. The super soft Malabrigo wool yarn will provide you with a warm and cozy accessory.

MATERIALS

Knitting loom

100-peg regular gauge knitting loom. Sample was knit using a Décor Accents baby afghan loom.

Yarn

[5] 600 yards (548 m) bulky weight yarn. [Malabrigo Chunky, 100% merino wool, in Tuareg, 104 yds (95 m) per 3.5 oz (100 g), was used in sample]

Notions

Tapestry needle
Knitting tool
Cable needle

Gauge

5.5 sts x 7 rows = 2 in (5 cm)

Size

30 x 40 in (76 x 102 cm)

Pattern notes

Back Cross Purl (BCP): Slip 1 stitch to cn and hold toward the center of the loom (peg is now empty), knit the next peg, then move this loop to the emptied peg, place the stitch from the cn on the empty peg then proceed to purl it.

Front Cross Purl (FCP): Slip 1 stitch to cn and hold toward the front of the loom (peg is now empty), purl the next peg, then move this loop to the emptied peg, place the peg from the cn on the empty peg, proceed to knit it.

Hourglass Stitch Pattern— multiple of 8 sts

	8	7	6	5	4	3	2	1	
20	●	●	●			●	●	●	
		●	●	✓	⟨⟩	⟨	↘	●	●	19
18	●	●			●	●			●	●
		●	✓	⟨	●	●	↘	↘	●	17
16	●			●	●	●	●		●
	✓	⟨	●	●	●	●	↘	↘	15
14		●	●	●	●	●	●		
			●	●	●	●	●	●	13
12		●	●	●	●	●	●		
	⟨	↘	●	●	●	●	✓	⟨	11
10	●		●	●	●	●		●	
	●	⟨	↘	●	●	✓	⟨	●	9
8	●	●		●	●		●	●	
	●	●	⟨	↘	✓	⟨	●	●	7
6	●	●	●			●	●	●	
	●	●	●			●	●	●	5

● Purl RS: purl stitch

☐ Knit RS: knit stitch

✓⟨ BCP: see notes

⟨↘ FCP: see notes

Directions

Cast on 100 sts.
Row 1: Knit.
Row 2: Purl.
Row 3: Knit.
Row 4: Purl.
Rows 5, 7, 9, 11, 13, 15, 17, 19: k2, follow Hourglass Stitch Pattern to last 2 sts, k2.
Rows 6, 8, 10, 12, 14, 16, 18, 20: p2, follow Hourglass Stitch Pattern to last 2 sts, p2.
Repeat rows 5–20 until item measures 38 inches (96 cm) from cast-on edge.
Next row: Purl.
Next row: Knit.
Next row: Purl.
Bind off with basic bind-off method. Weave ends in and block to measurements.

Potholders: Waves Potholder

A set of potholders is a great way to give color a try. These make great gifts and a lovely way to add color to your kitchen or bath.

MATERIALS

Knitting loom

44-peg fine gauge knitting loom. Sample was knit using a Décor Accents fine gauge loom. Any knitting loom with pegs spaced at ¼ in (½ cm) from center of one peg to the center of the next peg may be used.

Yarn

(2) 140 yards (128 m) sport weight yarn (70 yards main color, 70 yards contrasting color). [Louet Euroflax Sport Weight, 100% Wet Spun Linen, in Caribbean Blue (MC) and Violet (CC), 270 yds (246 m) per 3.5 oz (100 g), was used in sample]

Tools

Tapestry needle
Knitting tool

Gauge

12 sts x 20 rows = 2 in (5 cm) in stitch pattern

Pattern notes

Use two strands held together as one throughout.

Welting Fantastic Stitch Pattern (11-stitch repeat):

Row 1, 3, & 5: Using A, purl.
Row 2 & 4: Using A, knit.
Row 6: Using B, *k2tog, k2, kfb, kfb, k3, ssk; rep from * (see side panel).
Row 7, 9, & 11: Using B, knit.
Row 8 &10: Using B, rep row 6.
Row 12: Using A, rep row 6.

Directions

Using A, cast on 44 stitches.
Prepare to work as a flat panel.
Work Welting Fantastic Stitch Pattern 4 times.
Work rows 1–5 of Welting Fantastic Stitch Pattern.
Bind off with basic bind-off method.
Weave ends in. Block lightly.

BREAKDOWN OF ROW 6
*k2tog, k2, kfb, kfb, k3, ssk; rep from *

Step 1 Remove stitch from peg 1 and hold it. Move stitch from peg 2 to peg 1. Place the stitch you are holding on peg 1 (2 stitches on peg 1).
Step 2 Move loop from peg 3 to peg 2.
Step 3 Move loop from peg 4 to peg 3.
Step 4 Remove stitch from peg 11 and hold it. Move stitch from peg 10 to peg 11. Place the stitch you are holding on peg 11 (2 stitches on peg 11).
Step 5 Move loop from peg 9 to peg 10.
Step 6 Move loop from peg 8 to peg 9.
Step 7 Move loop from peg 7 to peg 8.
Step 8 Move loop from peg 6 peg 7.
Step 9 Pegs 4 and 6 are empty.
Step 10 Knit the row. Treat the pegs that have two loops on them as one.

Twisted Ladder Potholder

You could make one, two or all three of these practical and attractive potholders for your home!

MATERIALS

Knitting loom

40 peg fine gauge knitting loom. Sample was knit using a Décor Accents fine gauge loom. Any knitting loom with pegs spaced at ¼ in (½ cm) from the center of one peg to the center of the next peg may be used.

Yarn

140 yards (128 m) sport weight yarn (90 yards main color, 50 yards contrasting color). [Louet Euroflax Sport Weight, 100% Wet Spun Linen, in Willow (MC) and Cream (CC), 270 yds (246 m) per 3.5 oz (100 g), was used in sample]

Tools

Tapestry needle
Knitting tool

Gauge

12 sts x 20 rows = 2 in (5 cm) in stitch pattern

Pattern Notes

Use two strands held together as one throughout.

Twisted Ladder Stitch Pattern:

Row 1: Using color A: k4, *TW, k3; rep from * end on TW, k4.
Row 2: Using color A: p4, *k2, p3; rep from * end on k2, p4.
Row 3: Using color B: k4, *sl2, k3; rep from * end on sl2, k4.
Row 4: Using color B: p4, *sl2, k3; rep from * end on sl2, p4.

Directions

Using color A, cast on 40 stitches. Prepare to work as a flat panel.
Row 1: Purl.
Row 2: Knit.
Row 3: Purl.

Work Twisted Ladder Stitch Pattern 14 times.
Repeat Row 1 and Row 2 of Twisted Ladder Stitch Pattern.
Next row: Purl.
Next row: Knit.
Next row: Purl.
Bind off with basic bind-off method. Weave ends in. Block lightly.

TW=LT=LEFT TWIST—OVER 2 STITCHES

Step 1 Remove stitch from peg 2, hold at back of loom.
Step 2 Remove loop from peg 1 and place on peg 2.
Step 3 Place loop from Step 1 on peg 1.
Step 4 Skip peg 1.
Step 5 Knit peg 2.

Bricks Potholder

Another colorful example of making a useful project fun. This potholder uses blue and green to add vibrancy to any kitchen!

MATERIALS

Knitting loom

40-peg fine gauge knitting loom. Sample was knit using a Décor Accents fine gauge loom. Any knitting loom with pegs spaced at ¼ inch (½ cm) from the center of one peg to the center of the next peg may be used.

Yarn

(2) 140 yards (128 m) sport weight yarn (90 yards main color, 50 yards contrasting color). [Louet Euroflax Sport Weight, 100% Wet Spun Linen, in Willow (MC) and Caribbean Blue (CC), 270 yds (246 m) per 3.5 oz (100 g), was used in sample]

Tools

Tapestry needle
Knitting tool

Gauge

12 sts x 20 rows = 2 inches (5 cm) in stitch pattern

Pattern notes

Use two strands held together as one throughout.

Brick Stitch Pattern:
Row 1: Using A, knit.
Row 2: Using A, purl.
Rows 3 & 4: Using B, k1, sl1, k3; rep from * to last 2 sts, sl1, k1.
Row 5: Using A, knit.
Row 6: Using A, purl.
Rows 7 & 8: Using B, k3, sl1, k3; rep from *

Directions

Using A, cast on 39 stitches.
Prepare to work as a flat panel.
Work Brick Stitch Pattern 7 times.
Work rows 1–6 of Brick Stitch Pattern
Next row: Knit.
Next row: Purl.
Bind off with basic bind-off method
Weave ends in. Block lightly.

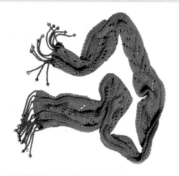

Table runner

An elegant table runner with a beaded fringe becomes a stunning central piece. Enjoy this simple yet beautiful design.

MATERIALS

Knitting loom

33-peg regular gauge knitting loom. Sample was knit using a yellow Knifty Knitter long loom.

Yarn

(4) 272 yards (249 m) worsted weight yarn. [Knit Picks Comfy Worsted, 75% pima cotton, 25% acrylic, in Whisker, 109 yds (100 m) per 1.75 oz (50 g), was used in sample]

Tools

Knitting tool
Beading needle to thread beads for fringe
Tapestry needle
600 seed beads (size 6 mm)
24 faceted rondelle Swarovski crystals (6 mm)
12 sewing pins

Gauge

9 sts x 10 rows = 2 in (5cm)

Size

8 x 66 in (20 x 168 cm), including fringe

Pattern notes:
One strand throughout.

Directions
Cast on 33 sts.
Rows 1–12: Follow chart. Repeat chart 25 more times.
Bind off with basic bind-off method.
Steam block to measurements.

BEADED FRINGE
*Space the sewing pins about ½ inch (1.27 cm) from each other along the cast on edge of the panel.
Cut 24 lengths of 12-in (30-cm) yarn. Tie a square knot at the end of the yarn. Using a beading needle thread 1 Swarovski crystal (so it rests on the knotted end of the yarn) and then slide on 25 seed beads. Secure the fringe at one of the sewing pins. Secure tightly with a knot. Weave in ends. Repeat 11 more times using the sewing pins as guides.
Repeat from * on the other end of the panel.

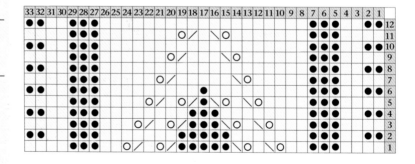

33	32	31	30	29	28	27	26	25	24	23	22	21	20	19	18	17	16	15	14	13	12	11	10	9	8	7	6	5	4	3	2	1	
●	●			●	●	●																				●	●	●			●	●	12
				●	●	●								O	/			\	O							●	●	●					11
●	●			●	●	●																				●	●	●			●	●	10
				●	●	●							O	/			\	O								●	●	●					9
●	●			●	●	●																				●	●	●			●	●	8
				●	●	●						O	/			\	O									●	●	●					7
●	●			●	●	●										●										●	●	●			●	●	6
				●	●	●					O	/		O	/	●	\	O		\	O					●	●	●					5
●	●			●	●	●									●	●	●									●	●	●			●	●	4
				●	●	●				O	/		O	/	●	●	●	●	\	O		\	O			●	●	●					3
●	●			●	●	●							●	●	●	●	●									●	●	●			●	●	2
				●	●	●			O	/		O	/	●	●	●	●	●	\	O		\	O			●	●	●					1

☐ knit
● purl
O yo
\ ssk
/ k2 tog

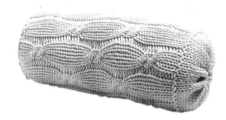

Bolster Pillow

An accent pillow for your home, knitted in a simple cable pattern. Cover up an existing bolster pillow or fill it up with polyester filling.

MATERIALS

Knitting loom

50-peg regular gauge knitting loom. Sample was knit using a yellow Knifty Knitter long loom and a Knifty Knitter loom clip.

Yarn

(5) 200 yards (182 m) bulky weight yarn. [Berroco Comfort Chunky, 50% Super Fine Nylon, 50% Super Fine Acrylic, in Oyster, 150 yds (138 m) per 3.5 oz (100 g), was used in sample]

Tools

Knitting tool
Cable needle
Tapestry needle
5 x 14 in (12.5 x 36 cm) neckroll pillow insert

Gauge

7 sts x 12 rows = in

Size

5 x 14 in (12.5 x 36 cm)

Pattern notes

One strand used throughout. Using the loom clip, set the knitting loom to a 50-peg configuration

Directions

Cast on 50 sts, join to work in the round.

Rounds 1–10: Knit.

Rounds 11: Purl.

Next 24 rounds : follow chart rows 1–24

Repeat last 24 rounds 2 more times

Next round: Purl.

Next 10 rounds: Knit.

Bind off with gather bind-off method.

Weave ends in and block lightly. Insert neckroll pillow.

Cut 24-inch (60-cm) length of yarn and thread through tapestry needle. Insert the needle through each of the cast-on edge stitches and leave them on the yarn. Cinch together and close the center hole with the remaining yarn. Weave ends in.

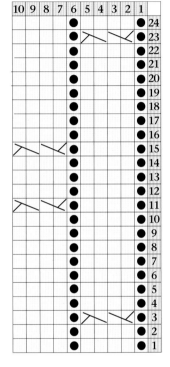

10	9	8	7	6	5	4	3	2	1		
				●					●	24	
				●	⤬⤬		⤬⤬	●	23	
				●					●	22	
				●					●	21	
				●					●	20	
				●					●	19	
				●					●	18	
				●					●	17	
				●					●	16	
⤬⤬		⤬⤬	●					●	15	
				●					●	14	
				●					●	13	
				●					●	12	
⤬⤬		⤬⤬	●					●	11	
				●					●	10	
				●					●	9	
				●					●	8	
				●					●	7	
				●					●	6	
				●					●	5	
				●					●	4	
				●	⤬⤬		⤬⤬	●	3	
				●					●	2	
				●					●	1	

☐ knit
● purl
 c4f

Couch Pillow

The couch pillow cover is a practical design that can be used to cover existing pillows to give your current decor a facelift. The buttons are ceramic decorative buttons.

MATERIALS

Knitting loom

100-peg regular gauge knitting loom. Sample was knit using a Décor Accents baby afghan loom.

Yarn

(5) 300 yards (274 m) bulky weight yarn. [Malabrigo Chunky, 100% merino wool, in Lettuce, 104 yds (95 m) per 3.5 oz (100 g), was used in sample]

Tools

Tapestry needle
Knitting tool
12 x 16 in (30 x 41 cm) rectangular pillow
3 buttons —1 in (2.5 cm) in circumference

Gauge

5.5 sts x 7 rows = 2 in (5cm)

Size

12 x 16 in (30 x 41 cm)

Seed Stitch Pattern:
Row 1: *k1, p1; rep from * to the end of row.
Repeat row 1.

Stockinette Stitch Pattern:
Row 1: K to the end of row.
Repeat row 1.

Directions

Cast on 52 sts.
Work Seed Stitch Pattern: 8 rows.
Buttonhole row: Maintain established Seed Stitch Pattern as you form the buttonholes. Work 8 sts in Seed Stitch, p2tog, yo, work 15 sts in Seed Stitch, yo, k2tog, work 15 sts in Seed Stitch, yo, k2tog, work the last 8 sts in seed stitch pattern.
Continue in established Seed Stitch Pattern until item measures 19 in (48 cm) from cast-on edge.
Next row: Work Seed Stitch pattern on first 10 sts, work Stockinette Stitch over the next 32 sts, work Seed Stitch on the last 10 sts.
Rep last row 43 more times.
Next 5 rows: Continue in Seed Stitch Pattern over the entire row. Weave ends in and block to measurements.

Assembly

Measure 2 in (5 cm) from the cast-on edge (the side with the buttonholes). Place a stitch marker at each side of the fabric. Fold the remaining fabric in half. Use mattress stitch to sew the sides. Position the buttons directly underneath the buttonhole openings. Secure buttons by sewing them in place.

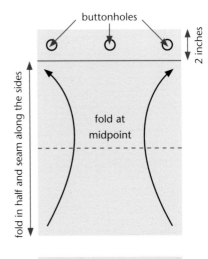

buttonholes

2 inches

fold in half and seam along the sides

fold at midpoint

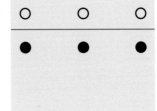

CHAPTER 9
Jewelry and Accessories to Wear

Princess Choker

Beads and lace are the perfect combination and they come together in this choker. It is a simple lace design with beads along the middle.

MATERIALS

Knitting loom

15-peg extra fine gauge knitting loom. Sample was knit using a Sett Sampler extra fine gauge loom.

Yarn

(1) 40 yards (36 m) fingering weight yarn. [Malabrigo Sock Yarn, 100% merino wool, in Lettuce, 440 yds (402 m) per 3.5 oz (100 g), was used in sample]

Notions

Tapestry needle
Crochet hook
Knitting tool
30 beads (size 11)

Size

12 x 1½ inches (30 x 3¾ cm)

Pattern notes

One strand throughout. A beading needle is recommended for threading the beads onto yarn.

Lace Stitch Pattern

Row 1: p4, k2tog, [k1, yo] twice, k1, sl1—k1—psso, p4.
Row 2: 4, 6, 8: k2, p2, k7, p2, k2.
Row 3: p4, k2tog, yo, k3, yo, sl1—k1—psso, p4.
Row 5: p4, k1, yo, sl1—k1—psso, k1, k2tog, yo, k1, p2.
Row 7: p4, k2, slide bead, yo,sl1—k2tog—psso, slide bead, yo, p4.

Directions

Cast on 15 sts and prepare to work a flat panel.
Next row: Knit.
Next row: Purl.
Next 8 rows: Work Lace Stitch Pattern.
Repeat last 8 rows until item measures 11 inches (28 cm) from cast-on edge.
Next row: Purl.
Next row: Knit.
Bind off with basic removal method. Leave a long tail.

Finishing

Block bracelet to finished measurements given.
With crochet hook, use tail from bind-off to work single crochet along bind-off edge as follows: Work along first ½ in (1 cm) of edge, chain 5; reattach yarn to edge and work single crochet along edge to ½ in (1 cm) before end of row, chain 5; reattach yarn to edge and work single crochet to end. Break yarn, draw through last st, and pull tight.
Sew pearl buttons to cast-on edge of choker, opposite buttonholes. Weave in ends.

Flower headband

A little bit of whimsy for your hair. Knit one or two, or even three, and add them all to a headband. Or you can attach them to clothing and wear as an accent piece.

MATERIALS

Knitting loom

10 peg knitting loom. Pink Knifty Knitter Loom was used in the sample.

Yarn

(4) 50 yards (45 m) worsted weight yarn. [Lorna's Laces Angel, 70% angora, 30% lambswool, in Powder Blue, 50 yds (45 m) per .61 oz (17.5 g), was used in sample]

Tools

Tapestry needle
Knitting tool
Beads or pearls to decorate the center of the flower
Headband of choice to attach the flower

Size

Depends on yarn weight used, Blue flower measures 5½ in in diameter

Petal Instructions

Make 5 petals
Cast on 10 stitches with yarn over cast on
Row 1-10: slip 1, knit 9
Row 11-18: Slip 1, k2tog, knit to the end of row (9sts rem)
Row 19: k2tog
Row 20: k
Remove item from loom with basic bind-off method.
Weave in all ends

Assembly

Thread tapestry needle with about 2 yards of yarn, take one of the petals by the cast on edge, pinch the two outer edges together thus forming a small pleat in the center of the petal, pass the tapestry needle through. Get the next petal and repeat the process. Repeat until all five petals have been joined together. Secure the five petals together, weave in all the ends.

Bead positioning: Thread a regular sewing needle with thread (preferably a color that is the same shade as the yarn). Attach a bead to the center. The sample has a pearl size 6mm at its center.

Once the flower is completed, simply sew it onto any headband. I recommend sewing a small piece of elastic to the back of the flower so it can be transferred onto other headbands.

Buttons Bracelet

Buttons can be used as embellishments too! Add style and character to your bracelets with a few pretty buttons.

MATERIALS

Knitting loom

7-peg regular gauge knitting loom. Sample was knit using a pink Knifty Knitter long loom.

Yarn

5 30 yards (27 m) bulky weight yarn. [Debbie Bliss Cashmerino Chunky, 55% merino wool, 10% cashmere, 35% microfiber, in Fuschia, 72 yds (65 m) per 1.75 oz (50 g), was used in sample]

Tools

Tapestry needle
Knitting tool
Optional—3 buttons in different sizes, shapes, and colors

Gauge

9 sts x 12 rows = 2 in (5 cm)

Pattern notes
Worked as a flat panel. Use a single strand throughout.

Directions
Cast on 7 stitches.
Row 1: *k1, p1; rep from * end on a k1.
Row 2: *p1, k1; rep from * end on a p1.
Repeat rows 1–2 until item measures 8 inches (20 cm) from the cast-on edge (or desired length). Bind off with basic bind-off method. Weave ends in. Block lightly.

Assembly:
Attach two small snap buttons to the wrong side of the bracelet to secure in place.

Optional embellishment:
Add three fun buttons to the bracelet.

Glamour Bracelet

The glamour bracelet is worked with a central cable that is decorated with swarovski beads and then the main focus is a big swarovski button.

MATERIALS

Knitting loom

10-peg regular gauge knitting loom. Sample was knit using a pink Knifty Knitter long loom.

Yarn

5 30 yards (27 m) bulky weight yarn. [Berroco Pure Merino Wool, 100% extra fine merino wool, in Storm, 92 yds (85 m) per 1.75 oz (50 g), was used in sample]

Tools

Tapestry needle
Knitting tool
Optional—5 Swarovski connectors and 1 flower-shaped Swarovski button

Gauge

9 sts x 12 rows = 2 in (5 cm)

Pattern notes

Worked as a flat panel. Use a single strand throughout.

Directions

Cast on 10 stitches.
Rows 1, 3, 5: p3, k4, p3.
Row 2: Knit.
Row 4: k3, c4f, k3.
Repeat rows 2–5 until item measures 8 inches (20 cm) from cast-on edge.
Bind off with basic bind-off method.
Weave ends in. Block lightly.

Assembly

Attach two small snap buttons to the wrong side of the bracelet.

Optional embellishment

Make the bracelet fun and personalized by adding buttons or Swarovski crystals. Sample shows 5 Swarovski connectors and 1 flower-shaped Swarovski button attached to bracelet with yarn.

Lariat Long Necklace

The lariat is one of my favorite pieces, wear unwound or wind it around your neck for extra warmth. The flowers at the end add a special touch.

MATERIALS

Knitting loom

11-peg regular gauge knitting loom. Sample was knit using a pink Knifty Knitter long loom.

Yarn

(5) (4) 40 yards (36 m) bulky weight yarn and 60 yards (55 m) worsted weight yarn. [Malabrigo Chunky, 100% merino, in Lettuce (A), 104 yds (95 m) per 3.5 oz (100 g); Malabrigo Worsted, 100% merino wool, in Fucshia, 30 yds (27m), in Buscando Azul, 15 yds (14m), and in Natural, 15 yds (14m), 215 yds (196 m) per 3.5 oz (100 g), was used in sample]

Tools

Tapestry needle
Knitting tool

CAST ON 3 STITCHES:

Insert crochet hook inside the loop on the last peg. Catch the working yarn, forming a new loop, place this newly formed loop on the adjacent empty peg. * Insert crochet hook in the newly formed loop. Catch the working yarn forming a new loop, place this newly formed loop on the adjacent empty peg. Repeat from * one l

Pattern notes

One strand throughout.

Directions
I-CORD

Using A, cast on 4 stitches. Work 62-in (157-m) I-cord over the 4 pegs.
Bind off with basic bind-off method and set aside.

ROSEBUD
(make 2)
Base
Using A, cast on 4 sts.
Rows 1, 3, 4: Knit.
Row 2: Cast on 3 stitches (see side panel). Bind off 3 sts with basic bind-off method. K3.
Repeat rows 1–4 four times more.
Bind off with basic removal method.
Assembly
Block. Join the side seam. Close the opening at the bottom of the base.
Petal
Using B, cast on 4 sts.
Row 1 & 3: kfb, k to the end.
Row 2 & 4: Knit to last 2 sts, kfb, k1.
Row 5–8: Knit.
Row 9: k1, k2tog, k to the end.
Row 10: Knit to last 3 sts, k2tog, k1.
Repeat rows 1–10.
Bind off with basic bind-off method.
Assembly
Block. Coil them from the long end with wrong side to the outside. Gather along straight edge and sew. Sew the bud to the inside of the base.

BLUE ROSE
Small petal
Using C, cast on 5 sts.
Row 1: kfb, k4.
Row 2: k4, k4b, k1.
Row 3: K7.
Row 4: K7.
Row 5: k1, k2tog, k4.
Row 6: k3, k2tog, k1.
Repeat rows 1–6 three times more.
Do not break yarn.

Medium petal

Row 1 & 3: kfb, k to end.

Rows 2 & 4: k to last 2 sts, kfb, k1.

Rows 5–8: Knit.

Rows 9 & 11: k1, k2tog, k to end.

Rows 10 & 12: k to last 3 sts, k2tog, p1.

Repeat rows 1–10 twice more. Do not break yarn.

Large petal

Row 1, 3, 5: kfb, k to end.

Row 2, 4, 6: k to last 2sts, kfb, k1.

Row 7–11: Knit.

Row 13, 15, 17: k1, k2tog, k to end.

Row 14, 16, 18: k to last 3 sts, k2tog, k1.

Bind off with basic bind-off method.

Assembly

Block. With wrong side to the outside, roll up loosely from the cast-on end. Stitch the straight edges together to form a flat base then push up center. Turn back petals and steam if necessary.

WHITE ROSE

Small petal

Using C, cast on 5 sts.

Row 1: kfb, k4.

Row 2: k4, k4b, k1.

Row 3: k7.

Row 4: k7.

Row 5: k1, k2tog, k4.

Row 6: k3, k2tog, k1.

Repeat rows 1–6 twice more. Do not break yarn.

Medium petal

Row 1 & 3: kfb, k to end.

Row 2 & 4: k to last 2 sts, kfb, k1.

Row 5–8: Knit.

Row 9 & 11: k1, k2tog, k to end.

Row 10 &12: k to last 3 sts, k2tog, p1.

Bind off with basic bind-off method.

Lariat Assembly

Seam rosebuds to each end of the I-cord. Seam the two roses to the I-cord about 12 inches (30 cm) from one of the ends.

Useful Information

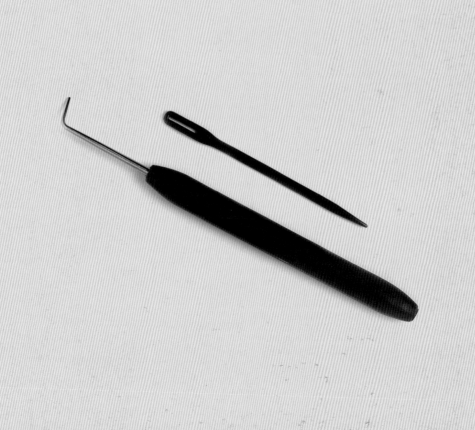

Useful Information

Reading Charts

Charts are pictorial representations of stitch patterns, color patterns, or shaping patterns.

Reading charts in loom knitting differs from reading a chart when needle knitting. In needle knitting, the knitting is turned after every row, exposing the wrong and right side of the fabric every other row. In loom knitting, the right side of the fabric is always in front, so we follow the pictorial chart as it appears.

- Charts are visual and pictorial representations of the stitch pattern. A chart allows you to see the entire stitch pattern.
- Charts are numbered on both sides, even numbers on the right side, odd on the left.
- Start reading the chart from the bottom.
- Each square represents a stitch.
- Each horizontal row of squares represents a row.
- Stitch pattern charts use symbols to represent stitches such as knit, purl, twists, yarn–overs, and any other stitch manipulation needed.
- Thick black lines represent the end of a pattern stitch repeat. The stitches after the black line are edge, or selvedge, stitches.
- Charts for color knitting differ from stitch pattern charts. In color pattern charts each different color square represents the color needed for that particular stitch.

- For Circular Knitting: read the chart from bottom up from right to left.
- For Flat Knitting: read the chart from bottom up from right to left on odd rows, and from left to right on even rows.
- Remember: the right side of the knitted fabric is always facing the outside. Knit the stitches as they appear on the chart.

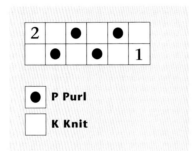

Chart reads:

For Flat Knitting:
Row 1: k1, p1, k1, p1.
Row 2: k1, p1, k1, p1.

For Circular Knitting:
Round 1: *k1, p1, rep from * to the end.
Round 2: *p1, k1, rep from * to the end.

A complete list of chart symbols and abbreviations used in this book is provided on page 140 (we are using needle knitting standard abbreviations and symbols whenever possible).

Washing your Knits

Hand washing is the best washing technique for all your knitted items. Even those items that were knitted with machine washable yarns can have their life extended by practicing good washing habits. Use a pure soap flakes or special wool detergent. Wash and rinse your item gently in warm water. Maintain an even water temperature; changing water temperature can shock your wool items and accidentally felt them. Before washing, test for colorfastness. If the yarn bleeds, wash the item in cold water. If the yarn is colorfast, wash with warm water.

Fill a basin or sink with water, add the soap flakes or wool detergent, using your hands, gently wash the knitted item. Avoid rubbing, unless you want the yarn to mat and felt together.

To rinse, empty the basin and fill with clean warm water, immerse your knitted item and gently squeeze out all the soapsuds. Repeat until all the suds are gone and the water is soap free. Pat as much of the water out as you can use the palms of your hands. Do not wring your item as this may cause wrinkles and distort the yarn. Place the knitted item between two towels and squeeze as much of the water out as you can.

To dry your item, lay it flat away from direct sunlight. Block again, if necessary, to measurements.

Head Size Chart for Hats

Once you have got the hang of making hats you will want to design your own, or convert the patterns here to your own ends. Use this chart as a guide only to the average head sizes to help you.

	Size	Circumference	Depth
Preemie	Preemie 1–2 lbs (0.45–0.9 kg)	9–10 ins. (23——25.5 cm)	3.5–4 ins. (9–10 cm)
	Preemie 2–3 lbs (0.9–1.4 kg)	10–11 ins. (25.5–28 cm)	4 ins. (10 cm)
	Preemie 4–5 lbs (1.8–2.3 kg)	11–12 ins. (28–30 cm)	4 ins. (10 cm)
	Preemie 5–6 lbs (2.3–2.7 kg)	12–13 ins. (30–33 cm)	5 ins. (12.5 cm)
Baby	Newborn	13–14 ins. (33–36 cm)	5–6 ins. (12.5–15 cm)
	Baby 3–6 months	14–16 ins. (36–41 cm)	6–7 ins. (15–18 cm)
	Baby 6–12 months	16–19 ins. (41–48 cm)	7 ins. (18 cm)
Children	Toddler	18–20 ins. (46–51 cm)	8 ins. (20.5 cm)
	Child	19–20 ins. (48–51 cm)	8 ins. (20.5 cm)
Young Adults	Teens	20–22 ins. (51–56 cm)	9–10 ins. (23–25.5 cm)
Adults	Adult Woman	21–23 ins. (53–58 cm)	10 ins. (25.5 cm)
	Adult Man	22–24 ins. (56–61 cm)	10 ins. (25.5 cm)

Hats need to be loom knitted with a 1 inch (2.5 cm) negative ease for a close fit, that is the hat should be slightly smaller when measured flat than the head it is to fit.

Common Abbreviations

[ ]	work instructions in brackets as many times as directed	dec	decrease	prev	previous
		diam	diameter	psso	pass slipped stitch over
( )	work instructions in parentheses in the place directed	ds	double stitch	rc	right cross
		ew	e-wrap	rem	remaining/remain
		foll	follow/following	rep	repeat
* *	repeat instructions between the asterisks as directed	FC	front cross	rev St st	reverse stockinette stitch
		fs	flat stitch/knit stitch	rnd(s)	round(s)
		g	denotes grams	RS	right side
*	repeat instructions following the single asterisk as directed	g st	garter stitch	RTW	right twist
		hs	half stitch	sc	single crochet
alt	alternate	inc	increase	sel	selvedge
approx	approximately	K or k	knit	sk	skip
BC	back cross	kbl	knit through back of loop. In looming this is created by e-wrap	skn	skein
beg	begin/beginning			skp	slip, knit, pass stitch over—creates a decrease
bet or btw					
	between	k2tog	knit 2 together—creates a right slanting decrease.	sl	slip
BO	bind off			sl st	slip stitch
but	buttonhole	l	left	ss	single stitch
CA	color A	lc	left cross	ssk	slip, slip, knit these two stitches together—creates a left slanting decrease
CAB	cable	lp(s)	loop (s)		
CB	color B	LT/LTW	left twist	ssp	slip, slip, purl these two stitches together—creates a left slanting decrease
cbs	chunky braid stitch	m	denotes meters		
CC	contrasting color	M1	make one. increase one stitch	st(s)	stitch(es)
ch	chain (use a crochet hook)	MC	main color	St st	stockinette stitch (knit every row)
cm	centimeters	mm	denotes millimeters	tog	together
cn	cable needle	mul	multiple	tw	twist stitches for a mock cable
CO	cast on	oz	denotes ounces		
col	color	P or p	purl	W&T	wrap and turn
cont	continue	p2tog	purl 2 stitches together—a right slanting decrease	yds.	yards
cr l	cross left			yo	yarn over
cr r	cross right			zip	zipper
dbl	double	pm	place marker		

Resources

Knitting Looms

The knitting looms used in this book were provided by two vendors, Décor Accents, Inc., and Provo Craft. If you would like to find a larger variety, do an internet search for knitting looms or loom knitting and you will find a larger selection at your fingertips.

Décor Accents, Inc.
www.dalooms.com
info@dalooms.com

Provo Craft
151 East 3450 North Spanish Fork, Utah 84660
www.provocraft.com

Yarn

Berroco, Inc.
14 Elmdale Road
PO Box 367
Uxbridge, MA 01569
info@berroco.com

Brown Sheep Yarn Company
10062 County Road 16
Mitchell, NE 69357

Crystal Palace Yarns
160 23rd St
Richmond, CA 94804
www.straw.com

Joann.com
2361 Rosecrans Ave
El Segundo, CA 90245
www.joann.com

Knitting Fever, Inc.
PO Box 502
Roosevelt, NY 11575
www.knittingfever.com

Koigu Wool Designs
RR#1
Williamsford, ON N0H 2V0
Canada
info@koigu.com

Lion Brand Yarns
135 Kero Road
Carlstadt, NJ 07072
Canada
www.lionbrand.com

Manos del Uruguay
www.rosiesyarncellar.com

Misti Alpaca
P.O. Box 2532
Glen Ellyn, IL 60138
www.mistialpaca.com

Muench Yarns
P285 Bel Marin Keys Blvd
Unit J
Novata, CA 94949
www.muenchyarns.com

Patons
P.O. Box 40
Listowel, ON N4W 3H3
Canada
www.patonsyarns.com

Plymouth Yarn Co.
P.O. Box 28
Bristol, PA 19007
pyc@plymouthyarn.com
www.plymouthyarn.com

Tahki Stacy Charles, Inc.
70–30 80th St. Building 36
Ridgewood, NY 11385
info@tahkistacycharles.com
1.800.338.YARN, Inc.

GGH
Distributed by Muench Yarns:
1323 Scott Street
Petaluma, CA 94954–1135
info@muenchyarns.com

Louet
3425 Hands Rd,
Prescott, ON K0E 1T0
Canada
www.louet.com

Online Yarn Suppliers

Malabrigo
www.malabrigoyarn.com

Berroco
www.berroco.com

Tilli Tomas
www.tillitomas.com

Kollage Yarns
www.kollageyarns.com

Index

Acknowledgements

As many of you know, a book is the work of more than one person. Although my name is on the front cover, the workload is shared by a group of talented individuals from around the globe. In one corner, you have the Quintet editorial team, my editor Anya Hayes and her team of technical editors, photographers, and models. In the other corner, you have me with an idea and a group of dedicated friends willing to lend a helping hand at a moment's notice. It is these two teams that have made the "idea" a reality.

I would like to extend a heartfelt thank you to all my loom knitting friends. Our journey has taken us through various stages in the loom knitting history. We have seen many changes and we have literally made history together. I appreciate all your love and your support. Throughout the years, you have shown me your kindness and your support through emails, letters, and even telephone calls. Thank you.

A special thank you goes to my friend Jill Watson—for her invaluable help throughout the completion of this book. For the many nights we spent together finishing off the projects. Friends come and go but you know a true friend is around when she sticks by you through many sleepless nights to finish the most needed baby blanket. Thank you!

Another world of gratitude goes to my friend Jennifer Stark, my wonderful loom knitting friend. Her keen eyes and attention to detail saved me from forgetting even the simplest bit of instructions. Thank you!

Quintet Publishing would like to thank the models: Clementine Anicet, Kasen Bell, Harriet Everitt, Cameron Frederick, Kerstin Heigl, Paul Mutagejja, Funda Onal, and Romilly Searle.